# BORN ON THE RIGHT SIDE OF THE TRACKS

# Born on the Right Side of the Track

A true story about an "out-of-the box" kid
stuck in an "in-the-box" world

Freddy Freundlich

Printed by Kindle Direct Publishing in the United States of America.

First printing, 2019.

ISBN: 978-1-7338955-0-7

www.rabbifreddy.com

To my children, the five greatest gifts the Lord

has bestowed on me:

Yael, Tamar, Yonatan, Danielle, and Adi.

**To be yourself in a world that's always trying to make you into something else is the greatest accomplishment.**

— Ralph Waldo Emerson

# Author's note

Everything you are about to read is true to the best of my memory. Almost all of the names in this book are real, although I have given pseudonyms to a few to protect both the innocent and the guilty.

This story is not about any particular nationality or religion. It is about people, good and bad, with most being a mixture of each.

# Foreword

In Judaism there's a belief that one who saves a single life is seen as if they have saved a whole world. By the same token, he who destroys a single life is considered as if he has destroyed a whole world.

While the Talmud may be referring to a physical life, humans are more than just physical beings. What exactly we are, I leave to theologians and scientists to debate, but I don't think there are many who will argue that there are both external and internal parts to human beings.

Whether we are talking about outer or inner parts (physical or spiritual), both parts go through a developmental process. This starts in infancy and continues into our adolescent years (and beyond). The two parts are inextricably entwined, and these years are known as our formative years. Nature or nurture, which has the most influence on these formative years? Most experts will agree that both have their place, but they will argue on which has more influence. While I do not claim to be an expert in these matters, I can only speak to you through common sense and my observations over the years.

When I look at little children, I see that for the most part they are all happy. They don't hold grudges, and even when they fight with one another, they make up and get over it quickly. It seems so natural for them to be happy, and I see no reason why this only has to work for children. It's remarkable that almost every scientific study I've seen shows that the majority of young children are happy, while at the same time most adults are not. We are talking here about the majority of the time, not specific time frames. So, what changes them? Nurture! Who's responsible for nurture? We are! Society, the all-knowing adults, each and every one of us is responsible. Whether you are a parent or a teacher, or if you have ever come across a child, whether for a short time or long, you have a very serious responsibility. You can save a world, or you can destroy it. The choice is up to you.

# Table of Contents

# Chapter 1

*Who am I, and where do I fit in this world?* —**Steve Jobs**

I've been running scared for most of my life. I still am, but today's different. I think pretty much anybody in my situation would be crapping in their pants right now. Even though I've been training for this moment, it seems surreal. I'm nineteen years old. I'm not just another grunt, I'm a combat medical specialist in the United States Army. At this moment, I'm scrunched up with about fifteen other guys in the back of an MC-130E Combat Talon. We're heading I don't know where.

This is the last place I'm supposed to be. After all, there's no draft, nobody put a gun to my head.

What am I doing here? What the hell have I gotten myself into?

Frank is sitting so close to me I can feel his heavy breathing on my neck. He's scared too. I can tell. I'm willing to bet everyone else in this plane is just as scared. None of us will ever admit it, though. We're all real men, much too tough to show fear, or any emotion. There are no windows in the back of this plane. It's shaking from side to side, and I've no idea if that's normal. I know we have several more hours ahead of us, so I close my eyes, trying to catch some shuteye, hoping that the whoosh of the aircraft engines will lull me to sleep. Instinctively, I know there's no way that's gonna happen. I'm trying not to think too much about what may lie ahead. Sweat drips down the curve of my back. I'm really very uncomfortable, freezing, even though we're dressed pretty warmly and packing a bunch of web gear.

I'm scared out of my mind.

I'm really not supposed to be here. Most of the people I know think I'm nuts for doing this, but I'm proud of myself. I'm doing something different, something patriotic, which is unusual in my social circles.

During and before the Vietnam war era, when the draft was still on, it wasn't uncommon for someone with my socioeconomic background to be in the United States armed forces. Nowadays, it's a real oddity. An all-volunteer army isn't for people like me, people born on the "right side of the tracks." We don't need to do this; we don't need the government to give us a leg up. Guys like me have all the odds in our favor of becoming successes.

Born the eldest of six kids in an upper middle-class home of educated orthodox Jewish parents, I had everything going for me. I went to private schools, summer camps, and was destined to go on to a decent university, probably an Ivy League school, like my parents did. After college I'd probably follow in their footsteps and become a businessman or maybe a doctor or lawyer. Mommy and Abba (Hebrew for father) were very successful, not just typically successful but out-of-the-box super successful. Amongst other things, Abba was a decorated war hero, from two different armies, in two different wars. After the war he went on to get his bachelor's and master's degrees. Mommy, a seventh-generation American, graduated summa cum laude from Barnard College and became one of the first women to own a stock brokerage firm on Wall Street. And as if that wasn't enough, she went on to become a medical doctor at the age of forty.

So, what happened to me? Why did most people feel that if I even got to eighteen, I'd probably be in a prison cell? What's so different about me? Was I born with some sort of a mental defect? Was I dropped on my head as a baby?

According to all the various experts (whom I refer to as the "Man") it was quite the opposite. They all agreed there was nothing wrong with me physically or mentally. In fact, according to them, I was extraordinarily bright. No, according to the Man, my problem was emotional. And I was lazy. Lazy and a troublemaker. They were sure I'd never amount to much. Mommy and Abba were constantly told that if they didn't find a way to "cure" their son of his chronic laziness, he'd end up dead or in prison.

Being that the Man is always correct, my parents were afraid. They loved me and tried everything they could think of to "cure" me, but my weird behavior only seemed to worsen, until one day the Man came up with an official diagnosis.

I'm emotionally disturbed.

So maybe the Man was right after all. Maybe today I'm going to die. But it won't be because I'm lazy, just out of the box. In fact, if I do get killed today, then I'll die a hero, and that'll show 'em.

# Chapter 2

*You can spend almost an entire lifetime just trying to forget a couple of minutes from your childhood.* —**Anonymous**

I love Sundays; the waft of blueberry pancakes coming from the kitchen is so overwhelming that the smell reaches all the way up to my second-floor bedroom. I jump out of bed and head downstairs where Mommy tells me to go out to the garage and tell Abba that breakfast is almost ready. I'm five years old and I'm the apple of my father's eye. He's so proud of me, and I'm so proud of him. I love to watch Abba working around the house. He can do anything, and he knows how to do everything. Whether it's working on the car, painting the house, fixing the plumbing, doing electrical work, or anything else, Abba knows how to do it. All this, even though his formal profession is teaching American History.

Abba's working on the car and I ask if I can help. Sure, he answers, go to my toolbox and get me the Philips head screwdriver. What's a Philips head screwdriver, I ask. Oh, forget it, I'll get it, he says. Abba loves me, I'm the apple of his eye, but I've let him down. It doesn't really matter that I try to hide my tears, because he's too busy to notice me. He's too busy finding the screwdriver.

Laurelton, New York, is a small middle-class village on the border of Queens and Long Island. We live across the street from the Laurelton Jewish Center and a couple of blocks down the road from the Young Israel of Laurelton synagogue.

I already feel like an outsider, not quite comfortable in my surroundings. I can't explain it to myself because I'm still only five, but somehow, I know I'm different. I live in a fairly typical Jewish middle-class home, along with my two younger sisters, Bethy and Dinny, (although eventually there'll be six of us) in a really nice three-bedroom, two-story, Tudor-style home on a pretty street. We have a great backyard with a swing set, a pool, and a barbecue pit. My father's a teacher with the New York City Board of Education, and my mother is a partner in a very successful stockbrokerage firm on Wall Street, which is pretty unusual in the early sixties.

"Walt Disney" perfect, I had just about everything I needed or wanted, which included attending private schools and summer camps, but I still felt as if I didn't belong. Partly because of my own peculiarities, but maybe also because my parents were so unusual. We never quite fit in with the "Joneses." Part of it was probably because their domestic roles were the opposite of the norms in our world, but it was more than that. Unlike most of my friends' mothers, my mother was never home to greet us when we came home from school. Mommy, a very busy businesswoman, wasn't involved in the PTA, the synagogue sisterhood, Boys or Girls Scouts, or the loads of fundraisers that were always going on. Not only that, when teachers or other parents wanted to speak with my mother, they would end up speaking with my father.

All my friends' fathers were the main breadwinners in their families, most of them businessmen or professionals. Abba was just a teacher who hated his job but loved the social benefits, and a big part of the social benefits were the hours. He came home early and had lots of days off, plus of course the entire summer vacation. Home a lot, Abba was always working around the house or on one of his many hobbies. He never seemed to have enough time for me, especially quality time. He was so busy doing something or another, or what he liked to call "stuff." His standard excuse was that being a home owner meant there was always something in need of fixing or improvement. One day he might be working on the plumbing or electricity, and the next day he would be painting the house. And he always seemed to be in the garage working on the car.

Abba, a very idealistic man, at best could be described as "nonpolitically correct." He seemed to make a point of being outside of the norms, whether because of his political beliefs or just his mannerisms. A big part of the orthodox Jewish world is weekly Shabbat prayer services at the synagogue. Every Saturday morning, we would attend, and almost always there would be a kiddush right after services. A kiddush is basically a small party, sponsored by one of the congregants to celebrate or commemorate an event of some sort. As a general rule, the whole congregation was invited, and in fact an announcement would be made at the end of prayer services explicitly inviting all the congregants to the kiddush. Everyone looked forward to these events because it was the perfect time to socialize. For us kids, it was especially loads of fun. Almost everybody was there. Except my father. Abba would say that he would only go when he was personally invited. He had this saying that "he was a private, not a general," and only generals accepted general invitations.

The truth is that, like most people, my parents were complicated, but in my case, I was the one that got hit with the ramifications of their baggage. Abba believed that daughters were the providence of the mother, and sons the providence of the father. That meant that my sisters were pretty much neglected when they came home from school, because Mommy came home very late. Abba, who was usually there when we came home from school, always seemed to be frustrated about one thing or another, and I seemed to bear the brunt of his frustration. I could never do anything right, and I never felt able to live up to his standards.

I was sure something was wrong with me. There were times, though, when he'd be so upset and I'd done nothing wrong, so I'd try and figure out what else it could be. Maybe it was his growing up during the years of the great depression. Or maybe it was growing up in a home where the multitudes of aunts, uncles, cousins, and grandparents were in the process of being murdered by the Germans. Who knows? It might have been for those reasons but was probably a combination of all sorts of things. One thing I do know is that my grandfather (my father's father) worked sixteen-hour days, six days a week and probably had very little patience for my father. Regardless of the reason, being his only son at that point, I bore the brunt of his frustration.

Even though he wasn't easy to live with, I was really proud of him. None of my friends could say that their fathers had volunteered in two different armies, in two different wars, and had been injured and decorated for bravery in both. One of Abba's strongest points was that he didn't just talk the talk, he walked the walk. First joining the United States Army in World War II and fighting in the Far East, he then volunteered to fight in Palestine for Israel's independence. Abba was extreme in everything he did and had no patience for the masses. His feeling was that they just went about their daily business without any real regard for the events surrounding them.

As he was off risking his life for God, country, and his ideals, his peers were getting their adult lives off and running. They started on their education, their marriages, and their careers. It can't have been easy for him, being a square peg person living in a round peg society.

Perhaps when he saw me following in his footsteps, it scared him.

When Abba met Mommy, it was love at first sight, at least for my father. He worshiped my mother from the first day he met her. But Abba was eleven years older and just a teacher and Mommy wasn't really interested. My grandparents (my mother's parents) were pressuring her to marry a professional man, like a doctor or lawyer. Nevertheless, my father persisted, and at the age of thirty-four married the woman of his dreams, a woman who was beautiful, brilliant, and highly successful at everything she did. As proud as he was of her, it couldn't have been easy for him, because he was suffering from what I guess could be called social discrimination.

# Chapter 3

*New beginnings come with much anticipation, especially for a child.* —**Anonymous**

Kindergarten was fantastic, and my teacher, Miss Gold, great! So naturally I'm excited to move on to the first grade, although I quickly realize that, as Dorothy said to Toto in the *Wizard of Oz* about not being in Kansas anymore, I'm not in kindergarten anymore.

I'm so proud and excited! The big yellow school bus arrives at the bus stop, and with my brand-new school bag and lunch box in hand, I'm now ready to take on the world.

I'm off to South Shore, a private Jewish school, where the school day is divided into two halves. First half is Judaic studies, with Rabbi Fabio as my teacher, and the second half general studies, taught by Mrs. Shawana. Daydreaming is probably my biggest passion, and all summer long I'd been imagining how wonderful first grade was going to be. And the first couple of days are indeed wonderful. After Jewish studies in the morning, we have lunch in the school cafeteria and then finish up the day with secular studies. Unfortunately, it doesn't take too long before I realize that the world is not exactly like Walt Disney.

During the 1960s, corporal punishment was the norm and was usually administered by your parents or, if you were really misbehaving in school, sometimes by the school principal. Since at the time it was still the norm, I don't necessarily fault anyone who used it, but Rabbi Fabio was unusually cruel.

Six years old, second week in first grade, and Rabbi Fabio doesn't approve of my behavior. I'm talking too much, he says, and not paying enough attention in class. Walking between the desks, he decides that I'm not following on the correct page as we're reading from the bible. Taking out his ruler, he cracks his ruler over my knuckles to get my attention. He gets my attention, and as much as it hurts, I bite my tongue and manage not to cry.

At home that night, I tell Abba what happened. He's not interested in what I've got to say. Instead, he's mad at me for not listening to the teacher. No excuses, the teacher's always right. I managed not to cry in class, but tonight, I cry myself to sleep.

I hate Rabbi Fabio and he knows it. I'm not the only one that he abuses, but I seem to be his favorite. One day, after I've really upset him, he calls me up to his desk at the front of the classroom, scolds me verbally, then pulls down my pants in front of the entire class. I'm shocked and petrified as he beats me on my backside using his ruler. He doesn't stop until it's red and raw. Once again, I manage not to cry, but the front of my pants is all wet.

I'm in pain, both physically and emotionally, but even worse, I've never been so humiliated. To add salt to my wounds, I can't complain to my parents, so I have to suffer in silence. I don't understand it. I'm not a bad kid. Never disrespectful nor violent, I'm just adventurous, and school is really boring.

Mrs. Shawana also has very little patience for me, but being a lady, she would never indulge in any kind of corporal punishment. She has her own way of humiliating kids she doesn't like. I admit it, I hate school! I'm bored and I talk to my friends during class. Mrs. Shawana doesn't like it and wants to make an example of me for future offenders. In the first grade, she says, we're here to learn. If you want to play, I'll send you back to kindergarten. That's where a kid like you belongs.

Mrs. Shawana, whose favorite punishment up till now has been having me stand in the corner of the classroom with my nose to the wall, now tells me to stand at the entrance of the kindergarten classroom. Being punished is never a pleasant experience, but this is really embarrassing. Miss Gold, my old kindergarten teacher who I love, sees me standing at the door and tells my sister Bethy to close the door. She says my being there is a distraction. Unbeknownst to Bethy or me, my fingers are in the jam of the door as she closes it. The pain is unbearable, but I don't know which pain is worse, the physical pain or the humiliation.

Most of the kids in my class get a weekly allowance of a quarter or fifty cents, and a few even get a whole dollar; I get one thin dime, that's ten cents. Rather, I'm supposed to get ten cents, but most of the time I'm being punished for one thing or another, so I usually don't get any allowance.

Labeled as a troublemaker, I'm not the most popular kid on the block. Even though the Man may think otherwise, I'm a normal kid and want to be popular. One morning on the way out of the house, I see Mommy's purse lying on the kitchen counter. Nobody around, I take out (steal) some money to buy candy. Not content with just small change, I decide to take a twenty dollar bill (at a time when a chocolate bar cost five cents) to buy candy from the candy machine at school. Between candy and soda, I pretty much empty out the vending machines. All I wanted to do is share my goodies with my classmates, but, stupid me, I had no clue that this would wave a red flag in the face of the school principal, who promptly call my parents.

When it comes to kids, there's no such law as "double jeopardy." I get punished by not just the school but also Mommy and Abba. The principal takes away my recess for a week, and my father gives me what is commonly referred to as a spanking. I don't know which is worse of the two punishments. Neither! In fact, the worst punishment is that I am led to believe that something is seriously wrong with me. Obviously, no other kid would ever dream of stealing money from their parents' wallets, so what's wrong with me?

After I've been at South Shore for another year, my parents decide they aren't happy with the school. For third grade, they move me to the Isaiah Day School located right across the street from our house. Isaiah Day School or South Shore, school's still school. Bored out of my mind and failing every class, I somehow still manage to get promoted up to the next grade.

As far as I'm concerned, the only good thing about school is that it keeps me out of the house, and during non-school hours I quickly learn to avoid my father as much as possible. One of the phrases that gives me some of the worst shudders is "I'm so glad you're home," because whenever Abba sees me, he always has some chore or another for me to do.

Like most kids, I hate doing chores, and mowing the lawn is the worst. Using a manual push mower for a kid is hard work, so when I mow the lawn, I like to take my time daydreaming about what life could be like, if only. Ever since learning to read, I've devoured every book I can get hold of. Some of my heroes are Mark Twain's fictional characters Tom Sawyer and Huckleberry Finn. Like them, I'm always getting into trouble just for being a kid, and my father is my worst nemesis. My daydreaming drives Abba crazy, and as far as he's concerned, I'm just plain lazy. Today he's especially frustrated with me because I'm supposed to be mowing the lawn, and he doesn't know that I'm currently in another world. Daydreaming about fishing for trout upstate, at Lake George, all of a sudden, I'm abruptly woken up from my happy adventure. Abba comes up from behind and shoves me to the ground. He yells at me that I'm a lazy so and so! The physical bruises healed...

**One of the skills I've learned as a parent is to give your kid an incentive to finish the chore. That way it's a win-win situation for everyone. For me there never was an incentive to finish the chore, and certainly not quickly, because there would always be another chore waiting for me afterward.**

Besides loving to dream, I've got one hell of an imagination, and I'm always looking for ways to turn my dreams into realities. Dreaming all the time about becoming a world famous explorer, every chance I get I'm exploring, inside or outside, with or without my bike. This is my escape from the Man. My imagination is my oxygen, my reason to live, and knowing that, there's always another exciting adventure around the corner.

# Chapter 4

*There's no limit to how complicated things can get, on account of one thing always leading to another.*
*—E.B. White*

Abba is a very idealistic man, a very black and white type of guy who doesn't understand that people are complicated, that nobody's perfect. This is especially true when it comes to his kids.

Maybe because I'm different, maybe because I'm a bit chubby, or maybe because I wear a yarmulke, I seem to make a great target for bullies. Two of the older kids in my neighborhood love to bully me whenever they see me, and I've programed myself to run in the opposite direction every time I see them coming. Usually they catch me riding my bike around town, but today I'm playing in my front yard when I see them coming down the block. I'm not scared because I figure they won't try messing around with me on home ground. For once I'm in the driver's seat, so, deciding to turn the tables, I start to taunt them. There's an old Chinese proverb about how anyone can start a war, but how it finishes is usually up to fate. Being on my own turf, I figure I'm safe, but my neighborhood bullies aren't interested in playing by my rules. They could care less that I believe that I'm on sacred ground. When they start chasing me, I race around to the back of my house, reaching the back door just in the nick of time. Or so I think. I see Abba looking at me through the window pane. I reach to open the door. To my chagrin, Abba looks at me and then calmly locks the door, leaving me still standing on the outside. The bullies catch up with me, beat me up, and leave me crying in my own backyard. My father later tells me that he locked the door to "teach me a lesson."

Even though I've failed every school year since first grade, they keep advancing me. Now nine years old and with no idea how, I'm in the fourth grade. Mommy and Abba felt that Isaiah Day School wasn't strong enough in Judaic studies, so they moved me to a new school, the Hebrew Institute of Long Island (HILI), in Far Rockaway.

Another year, another school, but my life is pretty much the same. I'm terrible in school, hate my father, and continue to be something of an anomaly. HILI is pretty much the same old same old, and once again, academically I'm pretty much of a disaster. I'm only at HILI for a year, but I manage to learn a very valuable lesson about not being quick to judge people.

One of my classmates is an outcast. Steven is very overweight, smells a little, is not very social and a terrible student. The one activity he really loves is playing chess. Not only does he love it, he's a fantastic player, and he teaches me how to play. Even though I'm not very good at it, I really like it and we play quite frequently. During our many games, which he almost always wins, I learn that although he's a bit odd, he's a really nice guy. The more we talk, the more I like him. He's very bright and interesting. I can't understand why everybody, including the teachers, feel he's so radioactive. Being that he's a social outcast, considered dumb and lazy like me, he spends his time doing nothing considered productive. (Nothing productive as far as the Man is concerned, but once again the so-called experts are wrong, this time very wrong! Just a few years later, Steven entered university and went on to become a very successful medical doctor. He was a child prodigy, and the system was too stuck in the box to see it, but thank God somebody finally did recognize it, saving his life.)

**I often wonder how many lives have been wasted because when they were kids, they didn't fit into the Man's box. How many lives could've been saved and changed, if these kids' talents were discovered in time and used, rather than perhaps them being thrown out with the trash?**

At nine years old, the one thing I've in common with almost every other boy my age is that almost all little girls are enemies. My worst enemy, my nemesis, is Sharon. Sharon and I have been enemies since kindergarten, and what makes our relationship even more complicated is that Sharon's younger sister Shelly is Bethy's best friend. One afternoon Bethy is over visiting at Shelly's house, and I drive over with my father to pick her up. Abba sends me up to the front door to get her. I ring the doorbell. My nemesis answers the door. While waiting for Bethy to come out, Sharon and I start taunting each other from opposite sides of the glass front door. Sticking our tongues out at each other, we do everything we can to upset one another. Suddenly, crash, bam, crash! I pushed too hard against the window, and I'm flying head first through the glass pane. Sharon starts crying hysterically. My arm and wrist have been cut badly, and blood is gushing all over the place. I'm scared, not because I'm bleeding heavily, not because Sharon has my blood on her face and is hysterical, but because I'm sure that Abba is going to kill me for breaking the window. Hearing the crash, Abba jumps out of the car and races up the walkway to the front door. He scoops me up into his arms and drives straight to the Long Island Hospital emergency room.

Lying on the gurney in the emergency room, all I can think is, thank God that I'm really hurt and in need of several stitches. If I hadn't been hurt, Abba would have surely killed me.

Laurelton is changing, like so many other neighborhoods in New York, and people are moving out. Most of our neighbors are moving to either Far Rockaway or the Five Towns area of Long Island. Mommy and Abba decide to move to Elizabeth, New Jersey, because in their words, why have to move twice?

I'm really confused. I know I'm a failure at school, but I'm still being advanced to the fifth grade in what will be now my fourth school. What's wrong with me? What difference does it make if I get good grades or not? No matter what, they're going to promote me. Does anybody really care?

Well, maybe things will be different in a new school and a new state.

# Chapter 5

*Change your place, change your luck.* —Jewish proverb

Our new home is amazing! While Laurelton was a lovely community, the Westminster section of Elizabeth is an upscale neighborhood, home to various business tycoons and celebrities. Our new house is huge, with four floors, six bedrooms, and five bathrooms on a beautiful half-acre plot. The main floor has a gigantic kitchen with a pantry, a cold room, and not only a formal dining room but also a breakfast room, a formal living room, and a study. Off the living room, there's a huge sun porch overlooking a fantastic backyard. The fourth floor, a finished attic, has two bedrooms, a full bathroom, and an extremely large storage area. Mine is the larger of the two rooms, twice the size of my old room, with our new maid, Teresa, in the second bedroom.

Elizabeth also means a new school, the Jewish Educational Center (JEC). I'm supposed to be moving up to the fifth grade, but because I'm a new student and my academic track record is, to say the least, not the greatest, the school administration decides to test my skills level. While up to par in general studies, they feel I'm lacking in Jewish studies. So, they decide that fifth grade is fine for general studies, but for Jewish studies I need to repeat the fourth grade. Who cares? I hate school anyway, so what difference does it make which grade I'm in?

Usually one of my parents drops me off at school, but whenever the option of walking presents itself, I take it. It's a beautiful October morning as I walk to school, playing with the leaves, enjoying the sights and sounds of the fall season. I don't walk briskly but dillydally along, enjoying my daydreams. It's almost two miles from my house to school, and I'm in no rush. I notice a dead squirrel lying in front of me on the sidewalk. On its fours, looking up at me, it occurs to me that we have science class today. I think to myself, what a great idea it'd be to take this squirrel to school; we can dissect it. Sure that my teacher and classmates will find it just as exciting and interesting as I do, I pick it up and wrap it in an old newspaper I found. My school bag full with all my stuff, I put the wrapped squirrel in my Superman lunch box, next to my peanut butter and jelly sandwich. Feeling very proud of my new acquisition, I continue on my way to school.

Good morning, Mrs. Danning, I say, proudly putting the paper bag on her desk. Look what I discovered on the way to school. She has absolutely no idea what the heck I'm babbling about and looks inside. Mrs. Danning is a nice woman but a typical establishment teacher. She really does mean well, but if you're a bit out of the box, there's really no place in her class for you. I'm not just a bit out of the box, I'm way out of the box.

Totally stunned by her reaction, I just can't believe what's going on. Is she having a heart attack? Maybe a stroke? She's really scaring me. Her face is all red and she's having a hard time breathing. She's freaking out and I'm frightened that something bad is happening. I need to get help—the police, paramedics, or somebody. But before I can figure out which way is which, she sends one of my classmates to find the principal, at the same time yelling for all the kids to evacuate the classroom.

This is the early seventies, long before shootings and terror threats were common in schools, but you'd have thought that I'd brought a bomb into school. The school is buzzing with excitement, but nobody other than Mrs. Danning has any idea what the crisis is all about. With all the commotion, someone pulls the fire alarm, and Rabbi Blau, the principal, along with his assistant comes running down the hallway telling the students to form two straight lines and immediately evacuate the building. Once he understands what the crisis is all about and that the building is not on fire, Rabbi Blau orders me to take the squirrel to the park across the street and dispose of it. Put it somewhere, anywhere, just get rid of it, and then report to my office immediately. Returning from the park, I'm so embarrassed. I just want to find a hole to crawl into, and then I hear the all-clear signal.

Here we go again. In this school just a couple of months and nothing seems to have changed. It's just like in Laurelton, but what did I do wrong? I just wanted to dissect a squirrel in science class.

I hate them all! Nobody understands me, not the teachers nor the kids. Everybody thinks I'm an oddball and a troublemaker. But again, what did I do wrong? The kids are all being taught to tow the establishment line, following in the footsteps of their teachers and parents. While adults are sometimes able to hide their true feelings, most kids aren't mature enough yet. They all laugh at me, especially the girls. I can't understand the teachers; weren't they at one time a child just like me? Don't they understand what it's like to be a kid? Perhaps they were raised in the same rotten system I'm in now. Even if they were at one time like me, it was probably beaten out of them by this same rotten system in which compliance to the Man is the only thing that's important. No one ever taught them what a childhood is really supposed to be about, such as in the stories of Tom Sawyer and Huckleberry Finn. Now all these former children act just like the *Borg* in *Star Trek*, having become part of the Man. They are destined to perpetuate the same system, passing it on to the next generation.

It's a beautiful Shabbat morning and as usual I'm walking to the synagogue by myself. I love walking in general, and on Shabbat in particular, because I feel less pressure. Taking my own sweet time strolling down North Avenue, I'm taking in the sights and sounds, the flowers and the trees. No rush, having a wonderful daydream about some adventure I'm in, when all of a sudden out of nowhere, Abba comes up behind me. This isn't the first time this has happened, but I didn't realize he was behind me; I thought he was already at the synagogue. For me it's déjà vu, for him it's once again me being lazy. Not happy with my walking pace, he gives me a shove to "encourage" me to walk faster, and I fall to the ground. This time it's not just grass but concrete pavement, and with my pants torn, I'm bloodied and bruised.

I hate him. In fact, I hate life! Not only am I misunderstood and a troublemaker, but no matter what I do, I'm also lazy!

An odd kid from an odd family is a great recipe for ridicule and low self-esteem, so I find that getting away from people and being all alone is my only real solace. My imagination is my energy, with the books I read being my fuel. I love to read, I love to explore, and the more I read, the stronger my imagination grows. There are many forests and old deserted houses in Union County where we live, and I'm drawn to them like a magnet, exploring every chance I get. School is boring. I find it a total waste of my time, but I've no choice because I'm too young to quit. I have however found one conventional activity that I like, in fact, one I love, and that's the Boy Scouts of America.

Boy Scout troop 613 meets at the JEC every Sunday evening, and in the winter it's already dark when we finish. Tonight, it's not just dark, it's very dark, and the weather is really terrible. It's been seriously raining all day, and because of the torrential rains, the Elizabeth River is overflowing and causing all sorts of traffic problems. North Avenue is partially flooded out because a tree has fallen into the middle of the street, and car traffic is now backed up for several blocks. Walking home in this thunderstorm, I get to the North Avenue intersection, and it's a complete mess, with the police nowhere in sight. Knowing my duty as a Boy Scout, I take it upon myself to help out. I start to direct traffic, helping the cars avoid the tree, and continue on for about an hour until the police finally arrive and replace me.

My parents, who know very little about my adventures, are shocked when the next day they see my picture in the *Elizabeth Daily Journal*. One of the drivers I'd helped was a photographer for the newspaper, who unbeknownst to me had taken a picture of me, all decked out in my Boy Scout uniform, directing traffic. The day after, my mother sees a letter to the editor written by the policeman who took over from me, mentioning me by name and praising me for being such a conscientious kid.

I'm suddenly a hero, but even an honor like this just seems to reinforce the notion that I'm a bit different. it's very difficult for me, because even though Mommy and Abba are proud of me, which may be a first, I don't want to be different. I want to be like everybody else. Today, being called out of the box is a compliment, but in the seventies, it was no compliment at all.

Being out of the box gets me in more hot water than accolades. I'm a kid and love being a kid. Why is it so hard for adults to understand? Not a bad kid, just the opposite, but nonetheless, I always seem to be in trouble. Whether it's the squirrel incident or my other escapades, it's always the same. Freddy's an oddball, a troublemaker; what are we going to do with him?

One of my favorite activities is playing cops and robbers, and what better place to play than on the school roof. For some reason, the Man doesn't seem to appreciate my sense of adventure, and no matter what I do, I always seem to freak them out. Yea, I know I broke the rules. I probably shouldn't have been playing on the school roof, but let's chill out a bit and put things in perspective. Instead, every little thing I do adds another notation in my file, and it's always my fault.

Doesn't matter who else is involved, it's always my fault, and as always, I'm accused of being the ringleader. This particular rooftop crime gets me suspended. Besides the suspension, there's also the whipping from my father, which is par for the course. But the biggest threat from the Man is what in their words is the biggest thing I should be worried about: It's now on my permanent record.

The first year at the Jewish Educational Center is a complete *Dr. Jekyll and Mr. Hyde* experience for me. On the one hand, I've had nothing but trouble with my fifth-grade classmates; they don't like me. On the other hand, I've had loads of fun with my fourth-grade classmates, who love me. Now that the school year's over, and even though I still did lousy, the school administration decides to advance me to sixth grade not only for general studies, but for Judaic studies as well. This however doesn't sit well with me, because I really like the younger kids and can't stand the older ones. I ask the school administration if I can stay in the fifth grade for everything, but they of course know better and say no. I figure one year won't make a difference in the big picture but having a good social life just might. At eleven years old, it makes sense to me, but the Man isn't interested in what I want or what's in my best interest; they have their rules and regulations. When I ask for an explanation, they look at me incredulously and answer, it just isn't done! They've no problem in embarrassing a kid by having him repeat a year, but God forbid if the same kid with good and intelligent reasons asks to be left back. Even with backup from my parents, who know I'd be happier, all they can say is they have "rules and regulations." Talk about in-the-box thinking but thank God this is one of the few times my parents back me up against the system. They insist, and I win!

My uniqueness continues into the sixth grade, and the final straw that gets everybody's attention is when I run away from home. As King Solomon was famously quoted as saying, "There's nothing new under the sun," and this quote is certainly true for me.

Every end of semester, I have a recurring ritual surrounding my report card. Rather, I should say, my failing report card, which I bring home and then show my parents. Punishment comes with a beating or grounding, and usually both. This time I don't know what's gotten into my head, but I decide to prolong my agony. It's Friday, and I'm scheduled to spend the weekend at Wayne's house. The fall semester just ended, and since once again it's report card day, I'm in no rush to go home. Of course, there are no surprises for me; same report card, same failing grades. I often wonder why they don't just make Xerox copies of my report card and use the same one over and over again. Returning home Monday afternoon after school, Abba is there to greet me. He asks to see my report card. I tell him I left it at Wayne's house. He looks at me and says, don't bother to come home tomorrow without it. Taking him at his word, I decide that I've no choice but to run away.

Sitting in Mrs. Swartz's class, with my pajamas and toothbrush already packed in my school bag, I'm racking my brain trying to figure out where I'm going to sleep tonight, knowing that the one place I can't be, and won't be sleeping, is at my house. Bingo, I've got an idea. After the final school bell rings, I quickly go to the bathroom and hide out till everyone has left the building. Being an avid explorer definitely has its advantages; I know the school inside and out. I probably know the layout of the school building better than most of the employees. Knowing where all the airducts lead to and how to navigate the various air conditioning vents, I also know which vent has the most crawl space. I figure I'll camp out for at least a week or so, until I can figure out my next move; it seems like a perfect setup. I figure that I'll stay in the crawl space during the day and come out at night. One of the vents leads right into a bathroom, so even during the day I can sneak out without anybody seeing me. Food is no problem either, because I can sneak into the school cafeteria at night, when nobody's in the building. I even have access to the school library. As I said, it seems like a perfect setup.

My parents naturally get worried when I don't come home after school. They call the school officials who in turn call the police. Being that I'm only eleven years old, the police are very concerned and start questioning everybody—my friends, neighbors, classmates, and even my sisters. By now everybody knows I'm missing. I've told no one of my plans, but my best friend, Avraham, who knows me pretty well, suggests that they search the school.

About eleven p.m., I'm up in the crawl space already dressed in my pajamas when I hear them: the police, my parents, and the school officials talking as they search the school. Because my new home has tunnels that navigate throughout the whole school, I'm able to track them all, listening in on their conversations as they conduct their search.

I've been cocky, but now I'm beginning to get really scared, knowing I can't live here forever. What am I going to do? They're starting to give up, feeling they've looked everywhere. Panicking, I know I've got to get out of this mess, and I need them to find me. I can't give up on my own because it will make me look like a fool, so I have to come up with a plan, and quickly. I can feel a panic attack coming on. I'm screwed. I can't believe the spot I've gotten myself into.

In retrospect, it's hard for me to believe that even in this situation I'd taken the time to brush my teeth and put on my pajamas, but habits are hard to break, whether they're good or bad.

Not knowing what else to do, I sneak down through the air vent into the gymnasium and start to move around, hoping to make enough noise that the search party will "discover" me, but as much noise as I make, nobody hears me. Now I'm really in a panic. I'm freaking out; they're getting ready to leave the building. Not knowing what else to do, I take a folding chair and throw it up against the wall, knowing that it will make enough noise that someone will have to come and investigate. Hearing the noise, the cops "find" me in my pajamas, "sleeping" in the middle of the gym, spot on center court.

During the drive home, nobody says a word. Mommy doesn't say a word. Abba doesn't say a word. Even worse, he doesn't even punish me. Now I'm really petrified. I just wish he would clobber me or something, but nothing! Not a word, not tonight and not for weeks after.

The following morning the last thing I want to do is get out of bed. I certainly don't want to see my parents, and I especially don't want to go to school. I know, though, that I've no other options, because I can't run away again. This is humiliating. I'm such a loser! If I didn't already have a reputation as a weirdo, now I'm totally finished. Nobody says anything to me, but I'm the laughingstock of the school and the entire community. If they didn't know before, now everybody knows what a total loser I am, children and adults alike.

# Chapter 6

***The secret of success is to be ready
when your opportunity comes. —Benjamin Disraeli***

I especially love detective stories and mysteries and dream of becoming a private detective when I grow up. My favorite series right now are the Hardy Boys and Nancy Drew mysteries. Being that I've pretty much read all of them, for my birthday, I'm introduced to the Encyclopedia Brown detective stories, and get a whole bunch of them to read.

But why wait until I grow up? Why not become a private detective right now? One of my buddies at school is Joey Hartman, and he's the only one that I can share these crazy dreams with. I ask Joey to be my partner, and we open up the Freundlich-Hartman Detective Agency, an official detective agency. The reason I can say we're official is because we saw an advertisement in a comic book to buy return address labels for a total investment of twenty-five cents, and we ordered them. When the United States Postal Service delivers a letter to the Freundlich-Hartman Detective Agency, the agency becomes official because the postal service is an official arm of the United States government!

Today the stickers arrive, and I'm so excited. I plaster them all over my bedroom, and Joey does the same in his room. To my deep regret, the Freundlich-Hartman Detective Agency closes down almost as quickly as it opened, because Joey's family moves to a different state. Bummed, because I just lost my investigative partner and I'm now stuck with a thousand return address stickers, I find myself in a real dilemma. I still have my burning desire to become a real detective, so I figure that if I'm going to make this happen, I need some help. Taking out the yellow pages, I look up private detective agencies in Northern New Jersey. One finger at a time, I start typing out letters on my mother's Smith Corona Classic typewriter to all the detective agencies listed in the phone book.

My letters state that I'm very interested in learning how to become a private detective, and can I please set up an appointment to meet with them. Taking some postage stamps from my mother's desk, I deposit the letters in a nearby mailbox on my way to school.

About one week later I arrive home from school and Teresa, our maid, tells me in her broken English, Mr. Freddy, you got phone call. Mr. Nilsen's secretary left her number and said you call her back. Who's Mr. Nilsen, I ask? She just shrugs. Confused, and with no clue who this Mr. Nilsen is, I return the call. Good afternoon, Nilsen Detective Agency. How may I help you? We received your letter and would like to schedule a meeting between you and Mr. Nilsen. I'm not sure that they've any idea how old I am, and I'm certainly not going to tell them. We set the appointment for the following Monday. I have no idea who Mr. Matthew Nilsen is or anything else about the Nilsen Detective Agency, but I figure he must be a big shot. Being just eleven years old, I don't really grasp what's going on, but I get this feeling that something important is happening in my life.

The day of my meeting is fast approaching and I'm getting really nervous, so I ask my friend Harley to come with me. Harley doesn't really believe me when I tell him that I've an appointment with this hotshot detective, but he already knows that anything is possible with me, so he figures what the heck, he'll go along for the ride.

Monday afternoon after school, Harley and I ride downtown on our bikes to Broad Street in Elizabeth. Walking into this massive office building, we proceed to the front desk, look up at the armed guard, and ask where we can find Mr. Nilsen's office. The guard looks like possibly a former marine. He eyes us from his great height and asks, is Mr. Nilsen expecting you? With loads of bravado I say yes, we've an appointment! It doesn't take us long to learn that the Nilsen Detective Agency is the largest locally owned private guard service in the state, besides doing loads of investigative work. Mr. Matthew Nilsen is the founder and president of the company, as well as an elected lawmaker for the Union County legislature. As we are escorted through the building, everyone is staring at us trying to figure out who the heck these two little kids with yarmulkes are. We're led into an enormous inner office, sort of like Scrooge McDuck's office, or the Oval Office. It's huge, with a massive oak desk and some very comfortable and expensive looking leather armchairs for guests. There's also a beautiful credenza with a bunch of booze bottles alongside a picture of Mr. Nilsen and what looks like the president of the United States. As we walk in, Mr. Nilsen gets up from his seat, comes around to the front of the desk, warmly shakes our hands, and offers us a seat. I'm bewildered. Mr. Nilsen looks to me like a giant of a man, both physically and figuratively. I'm just a little kid so what do I know, but he definitely looks well over six feet, and he has the biggest and most genuine smile I've ever seen. He treats us as if we're visiting royalty.

Harley, who's just along for the ride, doesn't say much of anything, but he's just as flabbergasted as I am. Really getting into this, just blabbering away, I tell Mr. Nilsen about the now defunct Freundlich-Hartman Detective Agency, about the Hardy Boys, Encyclopedia Brown, etc., etc. Listening intently, Mr. Nilsen asks me all sorts of questions, just as if we're all adults in the room discussing a big business deal. He is particularly interested in our yarmulkes and wants to know what it means to be an orthodox Jew. We really don't have a clue how to answer that, so we just focus on how we eat only kosher food and what Shabbat is all about.

Looking around the office, I'm soaking everything in. I keep pinching myself. Am I really here? Is this a dream? How can it be that Mr. Nilsen, an extremely busy man, is being so kind to us? It seems such a big waste of his time. After all, he could be discussing a business merger or even debating a new law, but here he is, taking his very valuable time to meet with two little kids who are total strangers to him.

After sitting with Mr. Nilsen for almost an hour, Maggie, his secretary, interrupts to remind him that he has another meeting he needs to get to. Thanking her, he tells her to please ask Raymond, the captain of the guard, to give these young men the VIP tour. Raymond, who's wearing a very sharp uniform with all the standard-issue equipment, including a really big gun, also treats us as if we're visiting dignitaries. As we go from office to office, Raymond explains about the different roles that people play here, and what each department is responsible for. This is a big place and a big operation with probably over a hundred people working here. During our VIP tour, beside visiting the different departments, we have our fingerprints taken, get to see all the different equipment, and then, as the tour is about to end, we're each given a mini gold detective badge.

With my official detective badge in hand, my body is tingling all over with goosebumps. I don't think I've ever been happier in my whole life! This afternoon is better than any super-duper ice cream sundae with all the toppings could ever be. The cherry on top is when Mr. Nilsen comes out of his meeting to say goodbye, asking us if we want a ride home. Thanking him but declining, we tell him that we rode our bikes. No problem, he says, and the next thing I know, we're being driven home in an executive black stretch Cadillac limousine, chauffeured by a uniformed armed guard, our bikes in the trunk of the car. The driver pulls into our driveway on Denman Place, and I see my mother looking out the dining room window. I imagine she must be having a heart attack, wondering what the heck a black stretch limo is doing pulling up to our house. When the chauffeur opens the passenger side door and I step out, her face goes white.

The next day in school I'm a bit of a hero because, thank God, Harley has a big mouth and tells everybody. While for a few days I am BMOC (big man on campus), it doesn't last long.

I don't know what Mr. Nilsen has in mind vis-a-vis a relationship with me after our first meeting, but as far as I'm concerned this is just the beginning. I start dropping by Mr. Nilsen's office every chance I get, and if Mr. Nilsen is there, he always makes time for me. Slowly but surely, I start to become a fixture around the office.

My appetite is growing, and I want to start buying my own stuff. Unlike most of my friends who get allowances, some of them quite a large amount, I get nothing. It isn't that my parents are necessarily against giving me an allowance, it's just that I'm always being punished for one thing or another. First and foremost, the fact that my school grades are a disaster means my first punishment is always "no allowance." I need to find a way to line my pockets, but what can an eleven-year-old kid do to earn money? There's got to be a way. I wish there was someone I could confide in and brainstorm with, but there isn't. Discussing any of my ideas usually gets me laughed at, or even worse, humored. I'm constantly made to feel like Don Quixote.

As there aren't too many employment possibilities for a kid my age, I've got to figure a way to create my own opportunities. Leafing through a business magazine, I see an advertisement offering an opportunity to sell commercial printing and advertising specialties. I fill out the coupon with my name, address, and phone number and send it in to National Press, Incorporated, located in Chicago, Illinois.

Once again it seems that no one cares how old I am, and they send me their catalogs. All I have to do is sell their stuff and they'll take care of the rest. I've now got my own business. I'm selling anything and everything that can have a corporate name or logo printed on it, everything from basic business cards, envelopes, and stationery to calendars, coffee cups, ashtrays, etc. My first two customers are my mother's stockbrokerage firm and the Nilsen Detective Agency. My business takes off super quickly and now I'm selling to anybody and everybody I know who has a business. My customers are even giving me referrals to their friends and relatives, because who doesn't like helping out an entrepreneurial kid? Besides, they're getting a good quality product and at a decent price. I really love having cash in my pocket, but even more of a rush for me is the excitement of having my own business and being a wheeler-dealer.

I'm starting to rake in the cash, but I'm also getting a bigger appetite, not just for the money but the real sense of empowerment in paying my own way. It's time to expand my business empire, so I decide that I want to be a newspaper boy. This involves a few challenges. To begin with, to be a newspaper boy for the *Elizabeth Daily Journal*, you've got to be at least twelve years old, and I'm only eleven. That's easy enough to remedy; I'll just lie about my age. The next challenge is a little more problematic. Being a paper boy means delivering the newspapers six days a week, which includes Saturdays, and this is impossible because my family is Sabbath observant. Always believing nothing is impossible, I go to the offices of the *Elizabeth Daily Journal* and explain to the circulation manager my challenge. I ask him if he'll sell me five newspapers at the vendor price, and explain my idea to go out, sell them, then come back for more. Without taking any money from me, he gives me the newspapers, saying, when you sell them, come back and then we'll talk.

I'm pretty sure he never expected to see me again, but two hours later I come back with the money, asking for more newspapers. My newspaper-selling venture starts off with me going door to door, asking the shopkeepers in the downtown area of Elizabeth if they want to buy a newspaper. Most of them say no, because they already bought their newspaper earlier in the day. But when I show up day after day, they eventually start waiting for me to come by, and slowly but surely, I build my newspaper route without ever having to work on Saturdays. Addicted, I begin to thirst for even more business, and while watching an old movie late one night, I get a great idea.

My brilliant idea is to mimic the old-time newsboys that I've seen in the movies. These are the guys who stand outside the train and subway stations, yelling Extra! Extra! Read all about it! So, every evening after finishing my afternoon paper route, I go stand outside the Elizabeth train station, selling newspapers to the commuters as they depart the train station. I'm now a fixture around Broad Street, and whenever I'm not at school or work, I look for any excuse to visit Mr. Nilsen.

It's almost summer vacation, and Mr. Nilsen offers me a job as an office boy. Being an office boy means running all sorts of errands around the office, getting lunch, coffee, and all sorts of other miscellaneous odds and ends. The truth is that what I am is a gopher: I go for this and I go for that. I'm so excited! This is my first formal job.

Till now, almost everybody I really know is Jewish, and usually orthodox. Now I'm getting to meet so many different types of people from so many different cultures. Mr. Nilsen's a WASP (white Anglo-Saxon protestant) which is totally alien to me; for Mr. Nilsen, this is probably the first time he's enjoying a close relationship with an orthodox Jew. Mr. Nilsen, who's old enough to be my father, has become a mentor to me in every sense of the word. He's involved in business, politics, and all sorts of civic activities, so even though I'm working at his office, I don't get to see him as often as I'd like. When I do though, it's always a great experience and often a life lesson. Besides Mr. Nilsen, I make friends with other adults in the office, who really seem to like me.

One morning after I get to work bright and early and after getting coffee and Danish for everyone, Maggie asks me to go through various boxes in the conference room and do some filing. She expects this job to take all day, but by lunchtime, I'm pretty much finished. I'm proud of myself; I'm definitely an eager beaver! Ken, one of Mr. Nilsen's two sons who's also a detective and works in the office, steps in saying how impressed he is about my conscientiousness, but he adds that sometimes when one has a job to do, you need to pace yourself. It's hard for me to understand what he's saying. After all, this is an adult and my boss, yet he's telling me to slow down, not to give it my all. After lunch is over, even though I've already completed the job, I realize I have to play like I'm working, so I return to the conference room. Bored, I start looking through the file cabinets, hoping to find something interesting to read. What I do find is a very interesting magazine called *Playboy*. Boy, was it interesting! A couple of hours later, Mr. Nilsen pops in to see how I'm doing and catches me looking through this magazine. I'm red in the face, so embarrassed. Mr. Nilsen laughs, gives me a big warm smile, and takes a couple of bottles of Coke out of the refrigerator. We have a long talk. No one ever had a conversation like that with me before. Thank you, Mr. Nilsen!

With summer now over, I've no choice but to go back to school (believe it or not I'm now in the sixth grade), but I still get to work part time for Mr. Nilsen. My special relationship with him is now not just between us but has stretched to our extended families. Besides Ken, Mr. Nilsen has another son, Ritchie, who's married, and of course Mr. Nilsen's lovely wife, Peggy. My relationship with all of them just gets closer and closer, but now it's not just between us. I introduce them to my parents, and they all instantly hit it off.

Besides being a very successful businessman and local politician, Mr. Nilsen is also well connected throughout the state. His family has lived in Union County for a long time, and as busy as Mr. Nilsen is, he's running for mayor of Elizabeth. Our current mayor is Tom Dunn and has been mayor forever. Even as a kid, I don't think Mr. Nilsen has much chance of winning. I don't care, and I'm working day and night for his election campaign. One afternoon, working after school, I'm at an intersection handing out "vote for Nilsen" bumper stickers when a stretch limousine pulls up. The passenger rolls down his window, and to my surprise, it's Mayor Tom Dunn. Very pleasantly, he asks me if Mr. Nilsen is paying me enough. More than you'll ever know, I answer. He smiles and drives off.

I'm no rocket scientist, but I'm right. Mr. Nilsen loses the election pretty handily, but not until I've had my first introduction into the political world.

My special relationship with Mr. Nilsen is not only good for me. During his campaign he's come to know my parents even better and has introduced my mother to the political world of New Jersey. This ends up being really good for both her and her business.

Christmas time is fast approaching, and this year I'm excited. Being Jewish, I never celebrate Christmas, but I've always loved the sights and sound of the holiday season. This year, I'll be buying gifts for Mr. Nilsen, his family, and a few other folks at the Nilsen Detective Agency. I know Mr. Nilsen appreciates good quality Scotch whiskey, so I decide that's what I'm buying him. Young and naïve, I'm so proud not only of my purchases but that I've paid for all my gifts with my own money, money I've earned. Christmas Eve, I head to the office to give Mr. Nilsen his gift. Maggie tells me that he's having lunch in the Carlton Hotel bar next door. Excited and with no patience, I saunter over to the bar and proudly go up to Mr. Nilsen, who's having lunch with a number of his colleagues. Merry Christmas, Mr. Nilsen, I say as I whip out the bottle of Scotch. Mr. Nilsen and his lunch guests have a good hearty laugh when they see me, and one of the lessons I learn that day is that even when intentions are good, bars tend to frown upon bottles being brought in from outside. Live and learn, something new every day.

Shortly after the new year I turn twelve years old, and Mr. Nilsen gives me a beautiful jade chess set as a birthday gift. Unfortunately, the Mr. Nilsen story is about to be overshadowed by my "real" life saga. I continue seeing Mr. Nilsen on and off for the next couple of years, and he is even an honored guest at my bar mitzva, but my life is slowly being taken over by the Man, and things are not heading to a good place for me.

For many years after, I would think about Mr. Nilsen's kindness to me and how much I loved him. I would often wonder what made him tick, why he would give so much of his time and energy for a kid he had no real connection with? I figured it was because he was a saint, just a really nice guy. There's no doubt in my mind that Mr. Nilsen was the best! His presence in my life gave me something very special, something I've always believed I could never repay.

# Chapter 7

*Man plans, God laughs.* —Old Yiddish proverb

I can't move. I really can't. In fact, I can't even get out of bed. There's a real throbbing pain in my ankle, and while there're no outward signs such as redness or swelling, it hurts like hell. My mother's sure I'm faking in order to not have to go to school, but every day the pain gets worse. When it spreads to my knee, Mommy decides to take me seriously and calls Dr. Berger, our family pediatrician. Dr. Berger comes to the house, examines me, and is stumped. He has absolutely no idea what's wrong with me, but he's worried and has me admitted to Elizabeth General Hospital for medical tests.

Even though I'm in loads of pain, I've got to say, I love being in the hospital. I'm treated like a king. Everybody is so nice to me. It's like a hotel: My meals are served in bed, I get to watch television whenever I want, and best of all, I don't have to go to school. The flip side is that they're always waking me up in the middle of the night to take my temperature, take my blood pressure, or stick needles in me. The daily routine is just as exhausting, with me undergoing all sorts of medical tests, but the pain keeps getting worse. Every test they perform comes back either negative or inconclusive, and the doctors are stumped. After spending more than a week in the hospital, they send me home no wiser than when I went in.

Because the pain is getting progressively worse, Dr. Berger refers me to a specialist in juvenile orthopedics. This new doctor also has no idea what's wrong with me, so he too admits me to the hospital for even more tests. I'm now a patient at Overlook Hospital in Summit, New Jersey, but once again, the tests are inconclusive. Another week in the hospital, and the pain's not only getting worse but spreading, and there's still no idea of what's wrong with me. More pain, more needles, more tests, but lots of tender loving care, food, and television.

Next referral is to a juvenile rheumatoid specialist at Mount Sinai Medical Center in New York City where I go through more of the same. It seems as if all hospitals have the same things in common: loving nurses, good food, and lots of television. I'm given every medical test they can think of, but still no answers. The only relief seems to be lots of painkillers and bed rest. Eventually the pain starts to subside on its own, until I'm eventually discharged with the diagnosis of having juvenile rheumatoid arthritis, which turns out to be a misdiagnosis, but that's for another story.

At Mount Sinai Hospital I get my first taste of real sadness. I become friends with Frankie, a really nice kid from White Plains. Frankie's in an adjoining room, too sick to get out of bed. Visiting with him a lot, I find out he's got a disease called leukemia. Not knowing what leukemia is, I believe him when he tells me he's almost better and that he'll be going home soon. Late one night, a couple of days before I'm to be discharged, I can't fall asleep. Tossing and turning, I faintly hear code blue on the intercom. Looking out at the hallway, I see a bunch of doctors and nurses running into Frankie's room. It's not long before I see them leaving his room accompanying a gurney. Sure that they're taking him to x-ray, I fall asleep, figuring I'll see him in the morning. The next morning, popping in to say hello to my friend, I find his bed empty. The room is empty and perfectly clean. I ask the nurse where Frankie is. He went home, she says.

I really didn't understand at the time why I felt so sad.

# Chapter 8

*Education is not preparation for life; education is*
*life itself.* —John Dewey

Not completely recuperated and with the school year pretty much over, I don't return to school. Throughout the years, my parents have continuously threatened that if my school work doesn't improve, they'll send me to the local public school. Always good to their word, they've now decided that this upcoming year they're ready to pull the trigger.

Alexander Hamilton Junior High School, while geographically not very far from my home, is socioeconomically a world apart. We live in the Westminster section, which is the most exclusive area in Elizabeth, and here nobody goes to public school. In our neighborhood everyone goes to Jewish or Catholic schools or one of the various prestigious private academies in the area. Most of the kids who go to Hamilton Junior High School are from the "other side of the tracks."

Seventh grade, once again a new school, and totally out of my comfort zone. With not enough worries in my life, I decide to make my life even more painful by continuing to wear my yarmulke in school.

From my first day at Hamilton Junior High, I'm constantly bullied. Since I'm no good at fighting, I've mastered the art of running, spending most of my days in flight mode. Life is pretty much unbearable, so I play hooky every chance I get, spending the day exploring the woods or hanging out at the public library. One of the constants in my life is my love for reading. Many days, I find myself borrowing books from the library, going to the forest to read, then returning the books the very same day.

Most mornings, my intention is to go to school, but when I walk out the door of my house, it seems that forces beyond my control pull me in the other direction. The other day, a truant officer catches me hanging out at the Bargain Town shopping center on Rahway Avenue and asks me why I'm not in school. As I'm wearing my yarmulke, I tell him it's a minor Jewish holiday and we have the day off. Of course, he has no clue one way or the other if I'm telling the truth, so he lets me go.

It's amazing! I can play hooky for days at a time, and no one's the wiser. That is, until one day when I particularly screw up. I decide that for once I'll go to school, but after a couple of class periods I can't handle it anymore, so I cut out for the rest of the day.

Mr. Golden, the guidance counselor for the seventh grade, is an extremely nice fellow who also happens to be a member of the synagogue my family attends. I really like Mr. Golden. He's one of the few adults that I feel cares about me, genuinely having my interests at heart. The day after I'd cut out from school early, I show up at school as normal, when Mr. Golden sees me. Where were you yesterday? In school, of course, where else would I be, I say innocently. Are you sure? According to my records, you were absent yesterday. Of course I'm sure, I say, I was definitely here yesterday.

Hamilton Junior High has been around forever and is an old four-story building with lots of stairs and no elevator. Mr. Golden, who has a bad leg and limps (I believe it was some sort of war injury) says he definitely believes me. For some reason, you were reported absent yesterday. Of course, I believe you were here, but I've got an obligation to check it out anyway. No problem, I say.

We walk up the stairs to the second floor, where he asks my first period teacher whether Freddy was in class yesterday. Checking her attendance roster, she says yes, he was present. I told you so! Mr. Golden responds, no problem, you know I believe you, let's just double check with your second period teacher. The only challenge is that my second period class is on the fourth floor. Mr. Golden and I, along with his bad leg, climb the stairs to my second period classroom. Mr. Golden asks my second period teacher whether Freddy was in class yesterday. Checking her attendance roster, she answers yep, he was in class yesterday. Once more, I say, see Mr. Golden, I told you so! There must've been a mistake.

No problem, I just have to be sure, let's just confirm one more time and that way everyone will be satisfied. My third period classroom is back on the first floor, so once again we climb down the stairs, and Mr. Golden with his bad leg asks my third period teacher whether Freddy was in class yesterday. This time, after checking her roster, she answers, no, according to my roster, he wasn't here yesterday. I look at Mr. Golden in total shock, saying, she's wrong! Of course I was here yesterday, she must've forgotten! No problem, Mr. Golden once again says, I believe you, let's just go and ask your fourth period teacher. Up we go again, this time to the third floor. Was Freddy in class yesterday? My fourth period teacher answers, no, not according to my records. I'm outraged, declaring my innocence, and insisting I was definitely in school yesterday. Mr. Golden doesn't flinch and says, of course I believe you, let's go and speak with your fifth period teacher.

At this point, looking at Mr. Golden's leg and knowing that we have to climb up all the stairs back to the fourth floor, I confess. She's right, they're all right, I actually cut out after second period.

It never ever bothered me that I'd cut classes or played hooky, but to this day I feel rotten about what I did to Mr. Golden. I wish I could've apologized to you, Mr. Golden, for making you climb up and down all those stairs, but now it's too late. I was such a jerk!

Mr. Golden was a rare and special man. Most of the adults during my childhood, whom I non-affectionately refer to as the Man, were part and parcel of the system. The Man always goes along with the party line, having no understanding of anyone who doesn't conform.

Similar to Mr. Golden, Rabbi Jaffee, the assistant principal at the Jewish Educational Center, was the only one there who tried to help or encourage me. Rabbi Jaffe was definitely an "in the box" type of guy, but he had a really good heart, constantly trying to convince my parents to change their mind about sending me to public school. Rabbi Jaffee never gave up, even when I'd already moved to Hamilton Junior High.

After a few months at Hamilton, Rabbi Jaffee eventually convinces my parents to try another school that specializes in kids who don't quite fit in the box. Conformity, then and now, is of paramount importance to the system, and anyone, especially children who don't conform, are considered special needs kids, and special needs kids need special needs schools. The biggest challenge with most of these special needs schools is that they're run by the same "in the box" educators who run the schools for the "regular" kids. This particular school that Rabbi Jaffee suggests to my parents is in the Crown Heights section of Brooklyn, New York.

Since things are really not working out so great for me at Hamilton, and both Mr. Golden and Rabbi Jaffe are pushing my parents, they decide they're willing to try out this new school for the upcoming spring semester.

In the meantime, I've my bar mitzva coming up, and I need to get ready for it. A bar mitzva ceremony is a really big deal in the life of a Jewish boy. At thirteen years old I will now be considered a man in the eyes of God. In the eyes of man, I'm also expected to take on more responsibilities, and one of these responsibilities is being able to lead certain rituals in the Shabbat services.

It's a bit hard for me to learn this stuff, since I'm no longer going to a religious school. Having nobody to teach me the various rituals, I ask Abba for help. What do you need help for? When I was a kid, I learned the Torah portion by myself. Convinced that once again I'm just being lazy, he begrudgingly asks my uncle who lives in Israel to prepare something for me. My uncle sends me a tape recording to guide me, which perhaps for others might do the job, but for me it just gets me more frustrated. I'm trying, I mean, really trying hard to learn the rituals, but it's just not working. My father keeps telling me that I'm just being lazy and not working hard enough. Worried that I won't get it right and that I'll make a fool of myself, I wish there was someone I can talk to. Feeling sorry for myself, I'm convinced once again that something's wrong with me, but I guess God feels sorry for me too and helps me out.

It's Friday morning, the day before the big day. Climbing out of bed and looking out the window, I see that it's snowing. Really snowing, blizzard-like snowing, and all the schools are closed. This sort of disappoints me, because I wasn't planning on going to school today anyway. That is, until I realize it's a Godsend. It's snowing so hard that on Saturday morning, the synagogue is half empty. This turns out to be really great for me, since I don't really know the Torah portion I'm supposed to be reading. This means, fewer people will be there and fewer people will laugh. My plan is just to wing it and hope nobody notices, and that's exactly what I do.

Thank God! I've made it through the rituals and now the festivities are about to begin. My grandparents, aunts, uncles, and cousins are all here for Shabbat, and tomorrow night, I'll have my big bar mitzva party at a fancy banquet hall in New York.

My favorite band is playing, my friends and relatives are here, and even Mr. Nilsen is here. For this one night, I'm in heaven.

# Chapter 9

*Never again.* —**Rabbi Meir Kahane**

According to Jewish tradition I'm now a man, but in the real world I'm still just a kid, and kids have to go to school. I'm now up to school number five, the major difference being that I'm living in a dormitory. Located on Eastern Parkway, in the Crown Heights section of Brooklyn, my new school is a dump.

Imagination is such a wonderful thing, one of God's greatest gifts to mankind. Unfortunately, real life sometimes gets in the way. I'd had such high hopes, thinking that things would be different here. I figured it had to be better; for one thing, I'm not living at home. In reality, things are now worse than ever. This place sucks! The school's terrible! The administration and teachers are scum and most of the students really rotten. This is a school that seems to prey upon parents, mostly from the modern orthodox Jewish community, whose kids don't quite fit in. Taking advantage of their desperation, they make unrealistic promises. To my despair, most of these kids are not just troubled but actually evil. I don't belong here and living with them in a dormitory is pure hell. My dream is now a nightmare, and life is miserable.

It's the kids, the staff, the buildings, and the neighborhood. Crown Heights used to be a beautiful upscale neighborhood with loads of fancy homes and mansions, but now, as in many such areas in Brooklyn, it's a slum, mostly tenements. The crazy thing, though, is that within Crown Heights there's a small upscale neighborhood surrounded by a larger crime-ridden area. This inner area houses the worldwide headquarters of the Lubavitch Chasidic community. The headquarters itself, where the Grand Rabbi resides, is at 770 Eastern Parkway and is the epicenter of the community. For a several-block radius around 770, you don't feel like you're in the slums. In fact, there are some very beautiful homes here, with quite a few successful people living in them. Our dormitory is right on the edge, between the two neighborhoods. Having to take the subway as the only way in and out of the neighborhood, I go through some very bad areas, which, combined with walking back to the dormitory, is always a risk to life and limb.

It's ten times worse than Hamilton Junior High, but somehow I've got to suck it up. One would think that it would be rather difficult to play hooky or cut classes in a dormitory school, but the truth be told, it's a piece of cake. I can actually cut school for days at a time and nobody knows, or if they know, they don't care. The only thing I can't do is play hooky overnight, which I'd really like to.

Every cloud has a silver lining, and mine's Duff. Duff is one of just a couple of students who don't have to live in the dormitory because he lives locally. Because both Duff and I are constantly playing hooky and Duff is not living in the dorm, it takes us a while to hook up. Once we do though, we hit it off almost immediately, becoming very close friends. Both of us hate school in general, and this school we find contemptible. We're hardly ever in school, cutting classes every chance we get, but now we each have a partner in crime. Duff and I are two birds of a feather, both totally out of the box, but he's in a different league than me. He's a year older, and he's a member of the infamous Jewish Defense League (JDL). Unbeknownst to the school administration and my parents, Duff invites me to become a member.

In a strange coincidence, the Jewish Defense League was founded by the late Rabbi Meir Kahane in Laurelton. It all started when one Halloween night a number of years before, the congregants from the Young Israel, which included my father, got together to protect the synagogue from hooligans. It seemed, and not just in Laurelton, that on All Hallows Eve, gangs of thugs thought it was open season to vandalize synagogues. That particular year, some of the congregants decided to fight back, and that was the origins of the Jewish Defense League. Therefore, when I attend my first JDL meeting, I meet a number of older kids who remember me from Laurelton, and they instantly befriend me.

Every chance I get, I go to meetings and self-defense classes. Part of the JDL's mission is not just to defend Jews but to destroy the stereotype of the wimpy Jew. The more I'm involved, the more my self-confidence grows. Within the JDL, there's a selective paramilitary group known as the Chaya squad (*chaya* means wild animal in Hebrew), whose mission is to do the dirty work of protecting Jews. Duff, along with his brothers, are part of the Chaya squad, and I'm invited to join. Sort of. The Chaya squad is made up of some very tough guys, almost all much older than me. I'm only thirteen, the runt of the pack, but everybody likes me, and besides, they need a decoy. Within the Chaya squad, everyone has a mission assigned to them. Mine is to be the official decoy, which means I'm a target, but I really feel like the mascot. Most important, I'm not yet a tough guy like they are, but I've stopped running every time I'm confronted by a bully. I'm in love with the JDL, the people, and the cause. Starting to become very active, I feel great. I feel at home. This is where I belong.

**Kids need a home, a place of acceptance. If you don't provide it to them, someone else will.**

Thank God, my favorite time of the year is here. The school year is coming to an end. For the first time in my academic career, due to their blissful ignorance, my parents are actually happy with me. The school, out of self-interest, tells my parents that I'm doing well, and I'm certainly not going to set them straight. They've no idea of the horrors I've had to endure over the past few months or the fact that I hardly go to classes. As far as my parents are concerned, ignorance is bliss.

The other thing that's making my parents really happy, or I should say, making my father happy, is that I'm involved with the Jewish Defense League. This is one of the few times my father's really proud of me. Despite all his faults, my father is a doer, not just a talker like most people are. He's a war hero who puts his money where his mouth is. Most people talk the talk, but my father walks the walk. He's experienced a lot and done some rather heroic things, almost dying in two different fields of combat. Once in the Philippines, when he spent a month in a field hospital, and then in the war for Israel's independence when he was hit by shrapnel from a hand grenade. In fact, when my father died at the age of ninety-two, he still had that same piece of shrapnel embedded near his heart. In 1947 it was too dangerous to remove it, and the doctors at the time felt he had a better chance of survival if they left it in. I guess they were wrong; it finally killed him about seventy years later.

My defending Jews makes my father really proud, so almost everything else takes a backseat. The most important thing to my father is that I'm getting a thorough indoctrination of Jewish values and history, plus self-defense lessons, all courtesy of the Jewish Defense League.

Now that it's summer vacation, I've started working again for Mr. Nilsen, and I find myself at thirteen years old involved in a sort of love triangle. Crazy as it sounds, I'm befriended by one of the women who works at the agency. I say woman, but even though she's married, Becky's only in her early twenties. Becky's marriage is not going well, and I guess it seems unthreatening to share your marital problems with a kid. Not necessarily true. We become really good friends, and she shares with me things that a thirteen-year-old boy has no business knowing or doing.

**I never, until now, confided in anybody about Becky. A combination of disbelief on my part at the time, and shame later, prevented me from ever talking about it. I guess writing this story has liberated me in some way, so, dear reader, there it is.**

My summer's busy. Between Becky, working for Mr. Nilsen, and continuing with my JDL activities, I'm not being lazy. Because Abba is happy with almost all my activities, he leaves me alone, more or less. The only time I ever see him is sometimes on Shabbat, but even then, I do my darndest to find friends to visit so I don't have to be at home.

Summer's much too short, and now it's back to the same old grind. Back to school and now I'm in the eighth grade. How the heck I keep being promoted is beyond me. I'm still in the same school of horrors in Crown Heights, with my routine of either not going to class or reading books under my desk continuing. But although I'm still in the same place, I'm a brand-new Freddy. Besides already knowing the system, I'm no longer Freddy the wimp. Boy, it feels great socking that son of a bitch in the mouth. I only wish I could be as cruel to him as he was to me. In fact, sometimes I even dreamt of being able to do to him and his thugs what they'd done to me last year, but I'm not built that way. One thing I now know is that nobody is going to bully me anymore. I hate bullies!

Being back in Brooklyn almost full time means much more Chaya squad action. After less than a couple of weeks, Duff tells me that we have a big action coming up, and my expertise is needed. The Chaya squad had gotten word of a gang of teenage thugs in Flatbush who were harassing the local Jewish residents, especially little kids walking home from school. Pleas to the local police get the same response, every time. Nothing can be done without proof or them happening to be at the scene of the crime in real time. Nobody ever likes calling the Jewish Defense League for help; we are outlaws, and the last thing law-abiding citizens want is to be affiliated with outlaws. Within the establishment, the JDL is, at best, a necessary evil, but the Chaya squad is a real pariah. That being said, desperate people sometimes do desperate things, and in a highly volatile situation, sometimes they'd ask for help. Many times, the victims are more afraid of the stigma of involvement with the JDL than the thugs. They would prefer to suffer in silence rather than call us. Rabbi Kahane, the JDL's mentor, always believed that when a Jew is in trouble, whether he asks for your help or not, you help him if you can.

In this case, the word "volatile" is being kind. The situation is so bad that young children walking home late in the afternoon from school are accosted and beaten up. The last straw is when a broken beer bottle is shoved down a young kid's throat and he almost dies. The Chaya squad decides to act, although, like the mafia, the Chaya squad has its ethics and needs to be sure that they are dealing with the real perpetrators. In order to get the proof they need, it is arranged that one evening, a chubby thirteen-year-old Jewish kid, wearing a bright green neon, crocheted yarmulke, will walk by the candy store where this gang, along with their girlfriends, hangs out. That chubby little kid is me. Drawn to me like bees to honey, the gang takes the bait. Far from being sweet, they come out of the candy store taunting me, when all of a sudden from both sides of the street come approximately twenty tough Jews. Wearing leather jackets, black motorcycle helmets with visors, and weapons in hand, the Chaya squad comes swooping down on these thugs. Like locusts, they beat the living daylight out of them. Funny thing is, these incidents have been going on for months, but after the Chaya squad's involvement, this gang never bothers Jews again. I play only a small part in these actions, but the Chaya squad always makes me feel as if I am an indispensable part of the team.

With the Jewish high holy days coming up, and even though it isn't mandatory, the school's encouraging the students to stay in school during the holidays rather than go home. Mommy and Abba, who are still in love with the school, believe that if the school encourages it, it must be good. Most of the kids go home, and although there are still a few of us here, no arrangements have been made for our accommodations. I decide that I've had enough of this place, and even though it's the middle of the night, I pick up and leave. My aunt lives in the Boro Park section of Brooklyn, about five miles away. To get there, I have to walk through Prospect Park, a pretty rough area at any time of the day but especially in the middle of the night. But I'm determined. Anything is better than staying in this place for the rest of the holiday. I've got to get out.

Walking through Prospect Park is a bit scary. It's dark, foggy, and drizzling, and I'm praying the weather is miserable enough that nobody's hanging out. Unfortunately, that's not to be, and I'm accosted by a bunch of thugs who see me as fresh meat. Feeling like a lamb surrounded by a bunch of jackals, I'm really scared. Hey bro, you got five dollars for us? I answer, sorry, I don't have any cash on me. All we find, all we keep, they say to me. That's not a question. I may be a little more self-reliant, and although I don't feel it right now, have a bit more self-confidence, but I'm no Bruce Lee. No way I can take on several adversaries at once, so, after kicking the gang leader in his private parts, I run like hell.

When I finally arrive at my aunt's front door, and after the shock of seeing me wears off, I tell her the whole story. I share with her everything that's been going on, or almost everything. After the holiday's over, she calls my parents. I never go back to that school again.

# Chapter 10

*We must always take sides. Neutrality helps the oppressor, never the victim. Silence encourages the tormentor, never the tormented.* —Elie Wiesel

Mommy and Abba were duped. No apologies are forthcoming to me, but begrudgingly they agree, this time it's not my fault. Nonetheless, with nowhere else to go, it's back to Alexander Hamilton Junior High School. Same school, same kids, but a totally different Freddy. I'm still wearing my yarmulke, and it doesn't take too long before one of my classmates walks up to me in the hallway and quietly whispers into my ear, Hitler was right. This obnoxious, cocky bully figures nothing's changed since last year. He remembers me as the quintessential prime target for every bully at Hamilton. This "brave young man" doesn't realize that times have changed and now his words are music to my ears. I guess he starts getting a clue that something's a little different when I literally take him by the neck and stuff him into a nearby locker. I feel awesome! Between him, and that son of a bitch from my last school, I'm on a real high! What a freaking unbelievable feeling! This is one of the proudest moments in my life, and the icing on the cake is that there's a bunch of girls witnessing this whole scene. They look at me in a way they never did before, and they're actually smiling at me. Last year, I was a laughingstock; now I'm a hero! I've never felt this way before. I feel like a stud. Not only are the girls actually talking to me, they're so happy someone finally dealt with this jerk. Wow, I'm blown away. What an unbelievable feeling.

I'm not the only one who's proud. Even though they won't say it outright, Abba and Mr. Golden are also real proud of me, I can tell. But rules are rules, and I have to be suspended from school for a week. It was definitely worth it, though, and I'll never regret it!

Returning to school the following week, I can't say that I'm exactly the most popular kid in school, but I've gained a certain respect, and more important, nobody ever bothers me again. Bullies don't like people who fight back.

Hamilton Junior High is now a bit of a different experience. I'm going to school most days and actually even enjoying a couple of the classes. In woodshop, I'm building a cherrywood coffee table, and although I've never been very good with my hands, it's actually quite exhilarating. For some reason, Spanish class also lights my fire. Otherwise, I find school as boring as I always have, but instead of playing hooky, I spend most of my time reading books in class. For some reason, it seems that everybody in the school is keeping an arm's distance from me, even the teachers. More of a ceasefire than a peace treaty, but I don't bother anyone, and no one bothers me.

Even at home, there's some type of a calm in the air. Mommy's not around much, Abba doesn't seem to be on my case quite as much, and I'm spending quality time with my sisters for the first time in quite a while. I've also been visiting Mr. Nilsen every chance I get. In a way it feels like I'm on some sort of vacation.

Living at home means living in New Jersey, which logistically makes my JDL activities a little more challenging. Challenging, but not impossible. I still manage, with the blessings of my father, to participate in JDL actions. Most of the actions are demonstrations, which for most of the participants are peaceful, but not for the Chaya squad. Still only thirteen years old, I'm racking up quite an arrest record, mostly for disorderly conduct, but sometimes they add in resisting arrest. Our primary targets for the most part are either the Soviet or Israeli governments. The Soviet government because the Iron Block is refusing to let out Jews who wish to emigrate, and at the same time making their lives miserable in the Soviet Union. A very popular cause right now, in fact for many a young Jew this is the cause celèbre of the seventies, similar to the protests against US involvement in the Vietnam War.

Many young Jewish people spend their Sundays in one way or another demonstrating against the Soviets, and most of these demonstrations are peaceful. The JDL on the other hand, do not want peaceful demonstrations. We want to make as much of a ruckus as possible, to gather media attention. This sometimes involves more serious actions, but for the most part I am involved in sit-ins and demonstrations. Some of these demonstrations get pretty violent, and on more than one occasion, I get hurt. Although our enemy is the Soviet regime, I never remember fighting with a Russian, but I fight many a time with the New York City police. One Sunday, the police have set up a blockade outside the Soviet mission to the United Nations, and we attempt to break through. I've no idea who throws the first punch, but the next thing I know I'm being chased by a cop. Eventually he catches and arrests me, but not before raining down on me a number of blows with his nightstick. Thank God, I'm wearing a motorcycle helmet, but I still have three fingers and my wrist broken. The crazy thing is that not only is this cop definitely not a Russian, he's for sure an American, and maybe even a Jew.

**As a kid you don't think of such things. All that matters is the knowledge that you're fighting for a good cause, plus of course the action. Definitely exciting days, but it makes me wonder looking back, where the heck were the responsible adults?**

Even with constant injuries of one sort or another, I never think about quitting. My next arrest is when I get caught smashing the windows of the Soviet Aeroflot Intourist building, but each time the JDL legal team takes care of me, and this is now part of the norm in my life. Even with all the arrests and injuries, there are a few humorous anecdotes. One Sunday before going off to my weekly JDL meeting, I have to make sure that I finish my chores, one of which is washing the dishes. Mommy had served fresh grapefruit for dessert, and in with the dirty dishes is a grapefruit knife. Late that night, I'm walking home from the train station after a JDL meeting in Manhattan, when an Elizabeth police department patrol car spots me. This not being New York City, the police consider a young kid walking around outside in the wee hours of the morning unusual and suspicious. Stopping me, they question and frisk me, and find the grapefruit knife. There were many times if I'd been frisked, the cops would've found real weapons. Switchblade knives, lead pipes, or even on occasion a gun, but tonight they find a grapefruit knife. For the life of me, I still don't know how it came to be in my pocket, but as far as I know, a grapefruit knife has but one purpose. I don't want to tell them I've just been to a JDL meeting, so I give them some cock-and-bull story as to why I'm out so late. I tell them I live in the neighborhood and am on my way home. This is all they need to hear, because if I am telling the truth and I do live in the Westminster section of Elizabeth, it means I am of prime stock and all will be good. If on the other hand, I'm lying, they'll arrest me for carrying a concealed weapon. Asking me where I live, they tell me to get in the car and we drive to Denman Place. It's well after midnight. My mother comes to the door, sees me sandwiched between these two cops, and expects the worst. One of the cops says, is this your son? Yes, she confirms. We stopped your son because he looked suspicious, and upon a thorough search of his belongings, we found a concealed weapon. Oh, my God, what was he carrying? This, the officer says, pulling out the grapefruit knife. Mommy, after getting over her initial shock and relief, suppresses her laughter. Thanking the officers, she says, I don't understand why he'd have a grapefruit knife with him, but don't you worry, officer, it won't happen again. If it's not one thing with me, it's another, but Mommy's relieved that it was only a grapefruit knife I was carrying, because she had some reliable suspicions that I had carried worse, much worse. The next day, she writes a letter to the editor of the *Elizabeth Daily Journal*, commending the two police officers on their diligence.

The Soviet Union is not the only government that has the wrath of the Jewish Defense League. Surprisingly, so does the State of Israel. Surprisingly because Israel is the Jewish state, but the government is very left wing, which means a natural antagonism between the JDL and the Israeli government.

Although we've had many a demonstration at both the Israeli embassy and consulate, this has got to be the craziest. Very big on our agenda is trying to convince the Israelis not to give away land. Our motto is "not one inch." The JDL has been holding demonstrations for weeks, which for the most part are peaceful. The JDL leadership wants to take it up a notch and decide that the Chaya squad would do their thing. While the "peaceful" demonstration is going on outside, a few of us manage to make our way into the outer lobby of the consulate in New York City. We sit down on the floor and refuse to leave. This action, known as a sit-in, usually has one purpose. Eventually the offending party will call the police and have the offenders forcibly removed and arrested. The interesting dynamics of a sit-in is that the demonstrators actually want to get arrested, while the victims don't necessarily want the negative publicity. So we sit, sleep, and eat in the outer lobby of the consulate, waiting to see who will blink first. Then the JDL leadership decides on what in retrospect is one of the craziest schemes ever conceived. The Israelis are known to have some of the best security in the world, certainly in their consulate facilities. While the outer lobby is considered outside of their security perimeter, getting into the consulate itself is a whole nother story. There are outer doors and inner doors, with lots of seen and unseen security. Supposedly the one kink in the system is a delivery entrance which when opened, leads straight into the consulate. The plan is that the four of us in the Chaya squad who are under sixteen will rush the guards, so we can set up another sit-in on the inside. Because we are minors, the JDL feel we can't get into too much trouble, but they don't realize that getting arrested might be the least of our problems. The doors open, we rush in, and the next thing I know there is an Uzi submachine gun literally against the side of my neck. I freeze. The Israelis, totally fed up, have us all arrested.

The next time I come up against a gun is even more harrowing. The actions of the Chaya squad are basically divided into two categories, political and self-defense. Self-defense on many occasions is proactive; in other words, we actively seek out the villains. On one such occasion, we become aware that some bad hombres who are attacking Jews hang out at a certain bar in the Canarsie section of Brooklyn. As we had done a number of times before, once again with me being the decoy, we set up these thugs. When we attack them, they start to run like scared rabbits, with Jeff and me chasing one of them into an apartment complex. Running in after him, we run straight into an ambush. Jeff yells, shotgun! All of a sudden, from what seems out of nowhere, I see a guy pointing a shotgun at us, letting go with a round of buckshot. I'm hit in the leg, actually hit by gunfire. Hurting like hell, I'm still able to get out of there. Thank God, it's only a graze, but it still needs to be looked after, and going to the hospital is out of the question. No problem, we have access to our own paramedic who takes care of me. It's only a graze, but at not quite fourteen years old, I'm way out of my league.

Meanwhile everything is still status quo, both at home and in school, but neither are very happy. Again, the experts have advised Mommy and Abba on a real good school, perfect for me. So here we go again, just celebrated my fourteenth birthday and on my way to school number six, with the dubious distinction of being in three different schools in the same school year.

# Chapter 11

*The difference between what we do and what we are capable of doing would suffice to solve most of the world's problems.* —**Mahatma Gandhi**

School number six. It's supposed to be a "really good school." They say it's the perfect place for me. Frustrated, my parents feel like they've no other options, so why not give it a try.

Yeshiva HH, located on Ocean Avenue in the Flatbush section of Brooklyn, is also a dormitory school. The difference here is that everybody has to live in the dormitory, no exceptions.

Mommy and Abba are hopeful that they've found the right place for me, and so far, so good. I'm also getting tired of going from one life to another, of changing schools every few months, so I decide I'm going to try really hard to make this work. As schools go, it's not so bad here, certainly not as bad as the last one. The kids aren't bad, the staff's okay, and the food is really good. Much to my chagrin, part of the reason it's a better school is because they're much stricter.

I'm no longer the same person I used to be. I'm no longer bullied or picked on. For the first time in as long as I can remember, I attend classes, participate in school activities, and basically keep my nose clean. Even though I live in the dorm during the week, I'm free on most weekends, so I'm still able to find time for my JDL activities. I'm on my best behavior, but the school is still far from happy about my extracurricular activities, although as long as it doesn't interfere with my schoolwork, they're willing to live with it.

The actions and demonstrations continue, and not only in New York. One weekend we're in some small town in Pennsylvania, demonstrating outside the home of a Nazi war criminal, and the next week we might be in Washington DC.

Apart from New York City, Washington DC probably has the most demonstrations in the entire country. Most demonstrations are straightforward and peaceful, but our group's mission, as always, is to make as much trouble as possible. This time our instructions are to handcuff ourselves to the White House gates, which doesn't sit well with the Capital police. Eventually the cops show up with bolt cutters, but we're doing everything we can to make it too difficult for them to actually remove the cuffs. "My" police officer is having a particularly hard time, and I'm not being very cooperative. Becoming very frustrated, she "accidentally" hits me in the head with the handle of the bolt cutter, knocking me unconscious.

Waking up in a Catholic hospital emergency room with a crucifix hanging over my head, I'm quite confused. Three days later I'm released from the hospital with a big bandage on my head, but all charges dropped.

Although in school I'm really on my best behavior, outside I'm always in one mess or another. My hospital stay made me miss school, and this not being the first time, the school administration's not very happy. I've had a number of these "accidents," but even though I seem none the worse for it, the Man is not happy. Getting arrested when underage really isn't such a big deal in the eyes of the law, within reason. The law is one thing, but my parents and the school administration are quite another. The school administration is really upset about my involvement with the JDL, and they only know half the story. I don't think my father is really that upset, but my mother for sure is not a happy camper. On the other hand, the JDL people are extremely happy. They know that because of my age, I can legally get away with almost anything, short of murder, and then who knows.

Regardless, I have a reprieve because the school year is coming to an end. Not knowing what my plans are for the summer, I hear that the Jewish Defense League has its own summer camp, and I definitely want to go. Mommy says enough is enough, but Abba convinces her that it will be good for me.

Camp Jedel is not a typical summer camp but is in fact a paramilitary training camp. Paramilitary boot camp for a fourteen-year-old kid is not just tough physically but also psychologically. The camp is supposed to be run by mature adults, but just like most military schools, it seems that the older kids are running the show, which is not the healthiest thing. We are woken up early in the morning by reveille and spend the day in nonstop training in advanced martial arts, proper use of weapons, and Jewish history. The idea is for us to become Jews to be feared. Although I start the summer already primed, I leave as a lean, mean, proud Jewish young man.

# Chapter 12

*Rebellion to tyrants is obedience to God.* —**John Bradshaw**

The first day of October 1975. Sitting in class in Yeshiva HH, still wondering what the heck I'm doing in the ninth grade. I've absolutely no interest in school but I'm feeling great because I'm all excited about tonight. All I care about these days are my JDL activities. I want to follow in my father's footsteps, just like he did thirty years before, because I know I'm fighting for a just cause.

Today there will be hundreds of people, if not more, demonstrating outside the famed Waldorf Astoria hotel in Manhattan. Idi Amin, the president and dictator of Uganda, is arriving. Idi Amin is persona non grata in the United States, but because New York City is home to the United Nations, any accredited diplomat to the UN is allowed to come to New York for any official UN business. He is scheduled to address the United Nations general assembly tomorrow, and the Ugandan mission to the United Nations is throwing a lavish party in his honor at the Waldorf Astoria. Not a very popular person in the western world, he's a brutal dictator and despot, so security for him is unusually tight.

The plan seems simple enough. All we have to do is elude the New York City police, hotel security, and the United States Secret Service. Who's we? Me and a few other underage kids. We're supposed to somehow find a way to get inside the hotel and then create havoc of some kind. Seems simple enough. What could be the problem? What's so difficult about creating havoc? By the way, what exactly is havoc?

Because of the planned demonstrations by various organizations, the area will be filled with lots of police dealing with crowd control. In addition, there will be quite a few plainclothes security officials, as well as the Secret Service and FBI. The last thing the United States government wants is a diplomatic incident.

I love the Jewish Defense League, but as usual, there's no real planning. Regardless, the five of us, all under the age of sixteen, are attempting to elude the police. We cross the barricades and manage to walk into the hotel lobby without being noticed, even though there are local cops and federal officers all over the place. Bravely and naïvely we attempt our infiltration, but before we can even get ten feet from the front door, all my coconspirators are stopped and busted. Somehow, and I don't really understand how, I walk right on in to the lobby of the Waldorf Astoria without being noticed.

I made it. I'm on the inside. I'm "in" the lobby of the Waldorf Astoria, one of the ritziest hotels in the world. Now what do I do? All alone with crowds of people who belong here and look the part, and me who doesn't. If I don't get out of here quickly, somebody is bound to notice, and I'll be arrested along with the others. I head for a nearby stairwell, go up a couple of flights of stairs, and find an unlocked utility closet in which to hide.

It seems like it's been hours, but all in all, it's probably only been about twenty minutes. Slowly starting to catch my breath and relax a little, I get my bearings. I feel a bit safer now. It doesn't seem like anybody is looking for me, so I'm free to complete my "mission." Create as much havoc as possible, but nobody told me exactly how. Especially now that everyone else has been busted, I don't know what I'm doing. All alone, I peek out of the closet, making sure that nobody's in the hallway, and inch my way out.

Starting to do a little exploring around the hotel, I head down the hallway and see a heat/smoke sensor. Armed with a cigarette lighter, I start a small fire in the ashtray, which immediately sets off the fire alarm. I've started to create havoc. While the hotel guests are coming out of their rooms to see what's going on, I take advantage of the confusion and slip into a nearby elevator. Up to the forty-seventh floor, I get out and, spotting a manual fire alarm, I pull it. My logic being that it will seem that the fire is spreading throughout the hotel.

I see some hotel guests running out of their rooms in panic. Not only are the fire alarms going off, but now the water sprinklers are starting to spray the area. In the pandemonium, I notice another utility room, this one much larger than the one on the lower floor. In this one there are all sorts of tanks, boilers, and electrical boxes. With my adrenaline racing and feeling a real high, I start pushing every switch I see and pulling every lever I can. Feeling like a secret agent fighting the communists in Eastern Europe, I'm working just from instinct. With no idea what I should be doing or for how long, I just keep pushing and pulling. Soaking wet from a combination of the water from the sprinklers, as well as my own sweat, I think that it would've been nice if my JDL superiors had been a little more specific about my job. Creating havoc sounds nice in principal, but what exactly do they want me to do? Should I try to actually set fire to the building?

Even though I've no real idea, creating havoc is exactly what I'm doing. I've created a real mess. People are running around in panic, sprinklers and alarms are going off. Due to fear of fire, the electricity grid has been shut down and the emergency power lights are now on. Idi Amin's reception is a disaster, and I guess I can relax because I've completed my mission. Later on, I'm told that men and women in formal wear were having to leave the party, some of them soaking wet from the sprinklers. The hotel guests are not exactly happy campers. As all this is going on inside the hotel, the outside is also turning into a real circus atmosphere. Besides the Jewish Defense League, there are multiple other demonstrations going on against Idi Amin, and with the mess I've created, the fire department and emergency services are having a hard time maneuvering through the throngs of people. What's really frustrating for the rescue and security personnel is that they're not even sure exactly what the nature of the emergency is. Most of the other groups demonstrating are considered mainstream organizations, and the last thing they want is to be associated with "radicals" like the Jewish Defense League, so they're trying to do everything they can to virtually and physically distance themselves from our crowd. The whole thing is a glorious mess.

I'm pretty sure that I've succeeded in my mission, but nobody told me what I'm supposed to do next. I sit there soaked to the bone, wondering what I'm supposed to be doing and what's waiting for me on the outside. Right now, all I can think of is how to get out of here, and however I do it, I need to do it quickly. Sneaking out of the electrical room, I'm expecting the ongoing pandemonium to give me some anonymity and a chance for escape. Quickly heading toward the elevator bank, I'm surprised when a man wearing one of those secret service types of earpieces steps out of the elevator. When he orders me to stop, I hesitate, but only momentarily.

One thing I do know is that getting caught isn't part of the plan. In a panic, I turn tail, running toward the stairwell. I don't think I've ever been more scared in my life. Down the stairs I run, the 47th floor, 46th floor, 45th floor, etc. Mr. Secret Service is right behind me, literally at my heels, yelling at me to stop in the name of the law. I keep going as fast as my legs can take me. Afraid to look back, I imagine him talking into his communications device, requesting assistance. My heart pumping and my adrenaline racing, I keep racing down the flights of stairs. With no thought as to where I'm going or what I'm doing, I just know I've got to get out of here. There are so many stairs it seems impossible, but what choice do I have? I can't use the elevators. Just as I reach the 39th floor, I see a giant of a man coming right at me. This guy is big, built like a brick wall. He also has an earpiece, which is probably not a good sign. With no time to even stop, I literally run smack into him. Talk about a head-on collision. Collapsing in front of this giant, I'm too dazed to move. This feels worse than any car accident I've ever been in. I must have at the very least a concussion, maybe even something's broken. Mr. Secret Service is right behind me and he's really upset. These guys are in no mood to politely arrest me. Young kid or not, they want to make sure I'm taught a lesson. They're going to make sure I never forget that one should never run from the police when ordered to stop. I don't even try and defend myself. I curl up in a fetal position and pray they'll tire of belting me.

My previous arrests were primarily for relatively minor crimes and misdemeanors, but this time it's a different story. Because of the beating they gave me, I'm really in pain. I hurt all over, especially my ribs, which I'm sure are broken. Feeling all alone, I know I'm in for some very serious charges. I'm trying not to, but I'm crying from the pain. In a daze, and unable to think straight, I vaguely hear them reading me my rights. In handcuffs, I'm dragged to the freight elevator, taken out through the hotel's service entrance, and shoved in the back of a van. I'm scared, in pain, and in a fog. And I have no idea what's going on elsewhere. I've no idea what damage has been done or whether anybody was hurt.

Instead of taking me to the local police precinct, they take me to the federal building. Never having been here before, I'm scared. Every other time I was arrested I was always with others, but now I'm all alone, with no uniforms in sight. Entering the building from a side entrance, we take the elevator, which seems to lead straight up to an interrogation room. Now that I'm a little more coherent, they read me my rights again and then leave me all alone, still in handcuffs. They've taken away all my belongings, and with no clock in here, I've no idea how much time passes. It seems to be about an hour or so, but who knows? Finally, what I perceive to be a couple of high-ranking officials come into the room, ask me if I've been read my rights and if I understand them. After my acknowledgment they proceed to question me, but they forget to ask me the most important question, which is how old I am. When I finally tell them that I'm just fourteen, they don't believe me. I do look much older than that, but if I'm indeed a minor, then it takes all the fun out of it for them. They've now got a problem! If I'm indeed just fourteen, then I'm a juvenile offender, which means they can't legally question me without my parents and lawyer present, and unlike an adult I cannot waive my rights. After this unsettling news, they leave me, still handcuffed but no longer behind my back, as they go check out my story. Waiting and sweating, I know I'm being observed from the two-way mirror. Eventually, someone comes into the room along with a couple of uniformed New York City policemen, and without saying a word they take me down to a patrol car. Amazing how much more comfortable I feel with the local cops rather than the federal guys. The cops take me over to the Midtown South police precinct, where I'm booked as a minor with a long list of charges. The charges are not just local charges but also federal, with two of my favorites being some federal statute that involves attacking a foreign diplomat, and the other resisting arrest. I may be guilty of everything else, but those two charges are bogus. Being that I'm under sixteen, I'm put into a holding cell all by myself. The wing I'm currently in is a detention area with a number of holding cells, and at first, I think I'm all alone in the entire wing. But even though I can't see any other prisoners, I start to hear voices from another cell, and it turns out to be a few of my JDL friends. These guys were arrested earlier in the evening and are all being held for disorderly conduct. Since they're all over sixteen, unlike me, they're considered adults, and even though disorderly conduct is a minor charge, they'll still have to post bail. They have no reason to worry, because soon the JDL lawyers will arrive and sort it out for them. Usually, under the age of sixteen is a magical age to be arrested, because short of almost anything really serious, you are nearly always released to the custody of a legal guardian.

I know I'm too young to actually have a heart attack, but I'm really shaking. Maybe because I'm still in loads of pain and not thinking straight, I'm not able to relax. I've always been assured by the JDL leadership that because of my age I've nothing to worry about, but right now, I'm worried!

Both the Secret Service and the police are not happy, but they've no choice but to release me. The only way they can keep me is if they can convince a juvenile judge that I'm a danger to myself or to others. The only other way is if they have no legal guardian to release me to, and this may in fact be a challenge for me. They tell me they can't get hold of my parents, and if they can't find a legal guardian to take custody of me, they'll have to send me over to juvenile detention. By this time, all my friends have been released and I'm back to being alone.

My ribcage is still really hurting, I'm lonely, and I'm starting to get really scared again. I don't know what finally happens. It could be that maybe they do get hold of my parents, who tell them I am currently living in a dormitory school in Brooklyn. Whatever the case, eventually both my school principal and dormitory counselor arrive at the police lockup to arrange my release. They're not happy either, and the next day I'm expelled. After less than two months in the ninth grade and my eighth school, I'm back home in Elizabeth.

I've been suspended on a couple of occasions, but surprisingly, even after six schools, this is the first time I've actually been expelled. Mommy and Abba despair, feeling that they've run out of options. It's not just that, I now also have my own challenges. Even though I was released from jail, it's a pretrial release, which means I'm out pending trial. Unlike my past arrests, which were usually summarily dismissed, this is serious business, and I'm worried.

# Chapter 13

*Extraordinary people survive under the most terrible circumstances and they become more extraordinary because of it.* —*Robertson Davies*

Mommy and Abba are in a quandary. What are they going to do with me? Expelled from school, with some serious criminal charges pending. Are there any possibilities other than a military or reform school? At this point, even Hamilton is not so easy to get back into, so for the time being I'm at home. The JDL is now off-limits to me. In fact, I can't even leave Elizabeth until this all gets sorted out. My parents are in consultation with the school officials, so for the time being I just need to keep my mouth shut and remain under the radar.

Since I love reading, I spend lots of time at the public library. Books have always been the perfect escape for me, and reading helps me dream about what life can be like, if only...

Before the whole Idi Amin drama, my parents had made plans to go away to some business convention for a few days. They send me to stay with my good friend Hugh, who lives around the corner. Even though Hugh's a bit older than me, we're really close. In addition to our slight age difference, we have a couple of other differences. Hugh's a good student and goes to one of the local prestigious private academies. I'm a bit jealous. Hugh seems to be living the life I've always dreamt of. His parents, whom I really love, are super fantastic. Hugh's father is a really cool guy, and about a year ago, he bought one of those old blacktop London taxicabs from an auction. Even though Hugh and I are too young to drive, we love hanging out in the car, where we spend hours discussing the meaning of life. It's not just the car; everything about Hugh's house is great. His basement is equipped with a ping-pong table, a pool table, a pinball machine, and he even has a soda fountain where we can drink as much Coke as we want. As cool as Hugh is, I'm one of his only guy friends, because he goes to a school that until only recently was a girl's-only school. He's the only guy in his grade and one of only four boys in the entire school. Besides hanging out in the taxi, our favorite activities are either hanging out at the Four Hundred Diner on Broad Street or taking the train down to the Jersey Shore, specifically, Asbury Park, where we spend the day on the beach and in the arcades on the boardwalk.

It's a really nice fall day in mid-October, and Mommy and Abba aren't due back until tomorrow. I'm enjoying every moment of their absence. Hanging out in the taxi cab, Hugh and I dream about how great it would be to get behind the wheel for real, to really go for a drive. We're just talking and then I get this great idea. Hey Hugh! My parents only took one of the cars on their trip, why don't we take the other one for a drive? We're looking at one another, sort of daring the other to really make a move. Neither of us are old enough to drive, certainly don't have driver's licenses, and never learned how to drive. What the hell, I say, it'll be fun, and nobody will ever know.

Knowing where Abba keeps a spare set of car keys, I grab them, and we get into the car. Key in the ignition, I slowly start to back the car out of the driveway. Hey Hugh, I'm driving a car, for real! Wow, I feel like a million bucks! But as we reach the end of the driveway, I glance into the rearview mirror and see a huge oak tree staring right back at me. Starting to panic, I search for the brake but it's too late. Crash! I backed up right into that tree. Freaking out, I get out of the car and look at the gash I've put both in the tree and the car. I'm beside myself! What am I going to do? I'm a dead man! Abba is going to kill me! Hugh is trying to calm me down, not having any clue as to why I'm so frightened. He tells me it's not so bad, don't worry, maximum, you'll be grounded for a few weeks. No, you don't understand, I tell him, you don't know my father, he will literally kill me! I feel as if there's now a mob contract on my head. My heart's pumping, my pulse is racing. What the hell am I going to do? Now Hugh's also starting to freak out. Not because of the car, but because of my reaction. He can't understand why I'm in such a state, but he realizes that I'm terrified. He feels for me but just doesn't get it. Hugh suggests we park the car back in the garage and act like nothing happened. In a total state of shock, I agree, not realizing that this is a totally moronic idea.

Friday afternoon, right before Shabbat, Mommy and Abba come home, and I return from Hugh's house acting like everything's just fine and dandy. For the next twenty-four hours I'm in a self-imposed living hell. It's one of the most stressful periods of my life, as I spend every moment dreading what I know is about to happen. It's the Sabbath, so there's really no reason for Abba to go out to the garage, but nonetheless, I'm still scared out of my wits. My bedroom is up in the attic, so I have a lot of distance both physically and emotionally from the rest of the family. It works out well for me in general because I love my space, but today more than ever, I really need my distance. I hunker down in my cave, too petrified to budge, waiting for the inevitable storm.

All of Friday night and throughout much of Saturday, I lie in my bed, too petrified to move. I find it hard to even breathe. The inevitable finally arrives at about three in the afternoon, when I hear feet (big adult feet) pounding up the stairs. Abba bursts into my room, his face red, his eyes bulging. He looks at me with a chilling, murderous look, while yelling and screaming about how he's going to kill me. I didn't need him to tell me. He starts beating the living crap out of me. The blows are fierce and harsh, and as soon as I can wrangle out from under him, I pound down the stairs, fearing for my life. Abba, enraged, grabs the nearest thing he can, which is a very large block of wood. He hurls it down the stairwell. Hit on my head and totally dazed, I lose my glasses. Even though I feel blood trickling down my face, I don't think there's any serious injury, but I know I've got to get out of here as quickly as possible; he's going to kill me! Starting to feel woozy, I make it down to the main floor of the house, stopping only to grab my shoes from the mudroom. Without even taking the time to put them on, I run down the street barefoot in the rain. As fast as I can and without looking back, I keep on running until I'm several blocks away. Stopping to finally catch my breath, I finally look back. It doesn't seem like he's chasing me, so I sit down on the curb and put on my shoes. I start to cry. Oh my God, what just happened? What am I going to do?

Not knowing where to go or what to do, I decide to try finding sanctuary in our local synagogue. Morning services were over a long time ago, and the evening services not scheduled to begin for a few more hours. I head over. I know where they hide the keys, and I sneak into the synagogue, knowing that nobody will show up for at least a couple of hours. Scared and shaking, I sit in one of the pews. It's hard to think because my mind is so cloudy, but what the hell am I going to do? My head is no longer bleeding. I can feel the dried blood. Maybe I have a concussion. No time to worry about that now, and besides, I'm certainly not going to the emergency room.

I know I can't go home, probably never can, but if not home, then where? The only place I can think of right now is my friends from the Jewish Defense League in Far Rockaway or Brooklyn, but that's in New York. How do I get there? I've no money with me nor any kind of transportation. I'm cold, wet, and tired, and sitting there I have another one of my crazy ideas. I know it's wrong, but I'm desperate.

Most of the congregants at my synagogue are Sabbath observant, which means that on the Sabbath they do not operate motor vehicles. Usually on Friday evenings before the start of the Sabbath, they drive their cars to the synagogue, leave the car over the Sabbath, and then drive home Saturday evening when the Sabbath is over. Common practice in many orthodox synagogues, some folks just leave their car keys in the synagogue for safe keeping.

Feeling as though I have no other choice, I go through the various pews until I find a set of car keys. My next step, on to the synagogue parking lot to figure out which car these particular keys belong to. One other thing, besides transportation, I also need cash. So, not very proud of myself, I rifle through the synagogue's charity box.

The parking lot is at the back of the building, and I go from car to car, trying to figure out which key fits. Bingo! It belongs to a black, beautifully clean and shiny 1973 Chevrolet Impala sedan. Looking around first to make sure that I'm still alone, I quickly get into the car. I start the car, petrified and remembering what happened the last time I tried to drive. With my entire driving experience up till now being less than five minutes, I very cautiously navigate my way out of the parking lot and slowly drive toward the exit. Inching my way out, I turn right on to North Avenue, the whole time trying to figure out exactly how to drive a car in general, and this car in particular.

No idea as to exactly where I'm going nor how I'm going to get there, I do know that I've got to get as far away from Elizabeth as possible. As I drive, I wonder what Mommy and Abba are thinking right now, but that'll have to wait. I don't know if it's physical or emotional, but I really don't feel well. I'm still woozy. My mind is in cobwebs. I've so many thoughts flowing through it that I'm completely confused. How am I going to get away with this?

This is nuts, I say to myself. Freddy, think about first things first. What's my most immediate need? To get as much distance from Abba and to avoid getting arrested. The only possibility is getting to New York City. Okay, next question. How am I, a fourteen-year-old kid, going to drive all the way to New York without anybody noticing? Even though I look much older, and in fact got an electric shaver as one of my bar mitzva gifts, I am still only fourteen. With no other choice, I decide to play it by ear. I'm not sure exactly how to get to New York, but since I've a general idea, I figure I can't get too lost. Following the signs, I cross over the Goethals Bridge to Staten Island, then continue onto the Verrazano Bridge into Brooklyn. Both bridges require a toll, and I'm very worried that when the toll collector sees me, the jig will be up. My fears are for naught, as no one gives me a second glance.

For the past forty-eight hours I've been petrified about one thing or another, and I'm still scared. Sure that at any moment I'll be caught and arrested, or even worse sent back home, I keep driving. The farther I get from New Jersey and my home, the less and less I worry.

Finally arriving in Brooklyn, I head straight to Duff's house. Telling him the story, I ask if I can hang out at his house for a few days until I can figure out my next move. No problem, he says. Of course, we lie to his parents, telling them that my parents are away for a few days and that I need a place to stay. I hang out at Duff's place for a few nights, until eventually his parents start asking questions and I know it's time to move on. My next stop is Shelly and Ralph's house in Far Rockaway. Siblings who, although both older than me, have become really good friends. Ralph is one of my closest JDL friends, and Shelly's like a sister to me. Shelly gets her mother to let me stay for a few days, but she stipulates only a few days.

These few days pass pretty quickly, and Shelly's mother says that it's time for me to go home. As far as I'm concerned, this of course is never going to happen. The next several nights I spend moving from one friend's house to another, but none of their parents are as hospitable as the first two, and I quickly have to move on. I'm out of places to go, so figuring that I've no other choice, I start living out of "my" car. It seems like a viable option, because I don't have to worry about anybody bothering me and I can stay for as long as I want. This is definitely true but would have worked out much better if it were spring or summer, rather than late fall. It's been getting progressively colder since I first ran away, and it's starting to get very cold, freezing in fact! Shelly, feeling really guilty that her mother won't allow me to stay at her house anymore, gives me a couple of blankets and some other essentials. At least I won't freeze to death.

Thank God for these blankets. It snowed all last night. I try to open the car door, but it just won't budge. The entire car has frozen up. The doors won't open, and neither will the windows. Even worse, the battery is dead so I can't even start the car for heat. Boy, am I scared. I'm trapped! I need to go to the bathroom badly, and I don't know what to do. Luckily, I find an empty bottle in the car. Having no other choice, I wait several hours until the sun starts to melt some of the ice, and little by little, I'm somehow able to get the window open and eventually climb out of the car to safety.

# Chapter 14

*Happiness is not something readymade, it comes from your own actions.* —**Dalai Lama**

Now that I've a place to sleep and transportation, I still need to find some cash for the rest of my needs. When I committed my cardinal sin of stealing the car, I understood I was already going to hell, so it didn't seem much of a stretch to also steal money from the charity box. Unfortunately, it was only enough to get me so far, but I did what I had to do to survive.

Now that I've acclimated myself to my new existence, I realize that being a thief is not the way I want to live my life, so I need to find employment. Looking much older than I really am, I've no problem getting a job at Kosher Country, a fast food restaurant located on the campus of Brooklyn College. The job and location work out great for me; I can park my "house" right next to my place of employment. I know it sounds crazy, but I'm really happy! Some nights I manage to avoid sleeping in the car by staying over at different friends' houses, but I always make sure not to outstay my welcome. This works out most of the time, but sometimes things don't go as planned. Always having my backup, I can always rely on my house on wheels.

Besides now having money in my pocket, going to work every day gives me a sense of freedom and stability. Being a fry cook may not seem like much of a trade, but I'm learning how to make all sorts of other food, not just French fries and hamburgers. I'm proud of myself. And although I'm surrounded by people much older than me, I seem to fit right in. One of the best perks of the job is that my meals are taken care of, and sometimes I can even take leftovers for the weekend. As unconventional as it may be, I've a place to sleep, hot food to eat, plus a really good social life. What more does a fourteen-year-old kid need?

Hanging out with Duff is always an adventure. His parents are some of the most wonderful people I've ever met, but they lost control of Duff and his brothers a long time ago. Their house is always chaotic, and I'm amazed how their parents haven't gone mad. Duff's bedroom is in the basement, and there's always something exciting going on, with all sorts of people going in and out. All of us are involved with the JDL, and martial arts and firearms are not just hobbies but skills that require constant training, and we don't slack on either. Especially when it comes to guns, we're serious players. Duff's basement wall is lined with mattresses, where he and his brothers have set up a real live firing range. It's unbelievable, and life's great! Most of my days are spent flipping burgers and cooking French fries, and my nights are either spent doing JDL activities or hanging out with Duff, or both.

In Elton John's song "Saturday Night's All Right," he sings that Saturday night is for fighting. But on a typically cold New York winter night, Duff and I have other things on our mind besides fighting. Like most Saturday nights, we're hanging out on the stoop outside his parents' house listening to music, when a couple of really cute girls from the neighborhood walk by. Duff knows Teresa vaguely, and she introduces us to Marie. We start talking, all really hitting it off, but we have one serious challenge. In this middle-class white neighborhood, there are primarily two types of people, Jews and Italians. Robert Frost was quoted as saying, "Good fences make good neighbors." For the most part that's exactly how it works here; in order to stay good neighbors, each side tends to stay to themselves. Neither side particularly appreciates their kids hanging out with the other. Since we're all very aware of this, we decide to go somewhere where we will be out of the way, in other words, where we can enjoy anonymity. Duff knows of an apartment building nearby with a perfect rooftop from which to view the moon and the stars. We're all in a great mood as we laughingly head over to the apartment building at the corner of Ocean Parkway and Avenue H. We take the elevator up to the top floor and continue up the stairs to the roof. Even though it's pretty cold, we manage to keep each other warm and have a great time just hanging out together, enjoying each other's company.

It gets kind of late and we're getting hungry, so we decide to head out to find something to eat. We gather up our stuff and head back to the rooftop door. Crap, it's locked. None of us realized that it's an automatic self-locking door. Uh oh, we're in trouble, big trouble! No problem, Duff says, we'll just use the fire escape. The four of us quietly start climbing down the fire escape, and as we reach the end of the steps, we find that the last part is a ladder. The ladder doesn't budge, either because it's rusted or frozen in place. This isn't good, and the girls are starting to panic.

Duff, being pretty agile, volunteers to scale down the side of the building. His plan is to come back up through the building and open the roof door for us from the inside. Great idea. We part company with Duff, and he climbs down to the street. The girls and I head back up to the roof. We're just about to set foot on the roof when an enormous gust wind comes out of nowhere. Losing my grip, I fall from the fire escape, tumbling down the stairs and crashing into Marie. Confused and dazed, I look over to see if she's all right, then find myself blinded by some sort of massive spotlight. I hear Marie crying, but before I can even move, I see a humongous helicopter hovering above with a spotlight shining directly on us. Then all of a sudden there are dozens of cops surrounding us. There's lots of noise, so I really can't hear them, but I see them shouting and pointing their weapons at us. Slowly the helicopter pulls away, the cops yelling at us to put our hands up and drop to the ground. I've no idea what's going on, and it doesn't help that the girls are freaking out. Marie, hurt from the fall and in hysterics, is grabbing on to me for dear life. Theresa meanwhile is screaming that her father's going to kill her. Even though I don't really understand why she's so freaked out, just hearing her saying those words sends a very uneasy chill up my spine. Thrown to the ground and handcuffed, I look up to see Duff being escorted through the rooftop door. He's also in handcuffs, and I feel like we're in some sort of war film. Now that the perpetrators (us) are securely detained, things begin to calm down. It's starting to snow so they take us inside the building where at least it's a bit warm. A police officer, who introduces himself as the precinct captain, comes over to question us. Before he even opens his mouth, the girls start yelling and crying that their fathers are going to kill them. Duff and I are looking at each other, and I'm wondering what the hell we did wrong, and specially to warrant a SWAT team with a helicopter.

The captain calms the girls down and explains what's going on. It seems that one of the buildings residents heard us walking around on the roof and was positive that a gang of criminals were perpetrating a home invasion on the entire building. Recently there'd been a similar crime, so when the police, already being on edge, received the emergency call, they took it very seriously. Not knowing whether to cry or laugh, Duff explains to the cop exactly what we're doing here and why we were on the fire escape. We're all worried for different reasons, and the girls are still sobbing, in and out of hysterical outbursts. I'm really scared because if we're arrested, they'll check me out and then I'm dead meat. How long will it take for the cops to find out that I'm a runaway and a car thief?

I have to admit, this guy's not a typical cop. He's actually a very nice guy and is trying to calm us all down. He says, I believe your story, but nonetheless you're all still guilty of criminal trespass, at the very least. Duff and I are dumbfounded but keep quiet while the girls continue with their nonstop pleading and crying. I guess their tears finally get to him, and he relents. Giving us a stern warning, he tells us if he ever catches us again, he will kick our butts, yadda, yadda, yadda. The telling point is that as he and the other cops are taking off the handcuffs, he looks directly at the girls and says, I'm only releasing you guys to prevent something much worse from happening. He adds that he knows who Marie's father is and is worried that if he indeed arrests us, he might end up having two to four murders on his hands tonight.

I'm sure he was only joking…

# Chapter 15

*Random acts of kindness, however small it may be, can transform the world.* —**Amit Ray**

We may have learnt our lesson about hanging out on rooftops, but that doesn't mean we stop hanging out altogether. So here we are again, another Saturday night, which means another party night for Duff and me. We're cruising in "my" car down Ocean Parkway heading toward the boardwalk in Coney Island when all of a sudden, I hear the whoop of a siren. Looking into the rearview mirror, I go into panic mode. It's a police cruiser. Okay, maybe he's on the way to some sort of emergency and just wants to pass me. This turns out to be wishful thinking, because I hear him on his loudspeaker ordering us to pull over. I guess I'm just a slow learner. Doing a quick calculation of the scenario and what the consequences will be if they do pull us over, I "put the pedal to the metal." Speeding recklessly down Ocean Parkway as they give chase, I've the vague hope that perhaps I can outrun them.

For a kid who's never had a driving license and only been driving for a couple of months, I'm doing okay in outrunning the cops. I actually may get us out of this mess. If it were only the one police cruiser, we might have a chance, but just like in the movies, they call for reinforcements, and now there are multiple police cars chasing us. Careening through the streets of Brooklyn (can't believe I haven't injured anybody yet) with the police in chase, my heart pumping and my adrenaline racing, I've the forethought to be concerned about Duff. New York City has crazy juvenile laws, and slight differences in age can make all the difference. Duff, who is older than me, is already on probation for some of his past JDL activities, and one more bit of trouble for him, there's a real good chance he'll be sent away to Spofford.

Spofford, which is located in the Bronx, is basically a kiddie version of Attica state prison, and not a nice place. It's one of New York City's juvenile detention centers and other than the fact that the detainees are minors, it's just as horrible as the most notorious adult facilities. Physically the place is decrepit, crawling with rats and roaches, sometimes even in the food. Besides being disgusting and unsanitary, it's a very dangerous place with the guards being more violent and criminal than the inmates. I know that no matter what happens, I need to make sure that Duff isn't caught.

Even though I've somehow taught myself how to drive a car, I haven't learned that a car needs liquids, lubricants, and various other services besides just filling up the gasoline tank. I've been driving this car now for a couple of months, and I've completely neglected everything apart from gas. At this stage, the brakes are in very bad shape. They squeak, and I have trouble stopping the car. Also, the car no longer goes into reverse. Whenever I need to back up, I just get out of the car and physically push it back. It's a total mess. I did have to replace a tire once when running off the road on the New York State thruway, but that's the extent of it.

The faster I drive, the scarier it's getting. The cops are right on my tail, and no matter what I do, they're right behind me; they're good. I just know I can't give up, but I don't know what else to do. All I know is we can't get caught, so I keep trying to outrun them, turning on to all sorts of side streets, trying to lose them. I'm terrified that I'm going to kill somebody, maybe even us. I keep looking for somewhere to stop the car where perhaps we can get away on foot, but every time I think I've lost them, another police car seems to come out of nowhere. I don't know how much longer this chase can continue, but suddenly my prayers seem to be answered. Looking through the rearview mirror, for the first time, I don't see any blue lights.

Trying to slow down, my foot goes straight to the floor. I keep pumping the brakes, but the car just won't slow down. Perhaps riding them like I have has made them even worse. Duff, I say, when we make the next turn, you need to jump out and run like hell. Making the turn onto East 35th Street, I'm about to slow down when I see a glimpse of a blue flashing light in my rearview mirror. It's too late to change plans, so Duff jumps out, and I immediately put my foot on the gas, speeding up again. We luck out. The cops didn't see that Duff jumped out, and the chase continues. With the cops still thinking that there are the two of us in the car, I run a red light. Turning right onto Coney Island Avenue, I'm momentarily distracted by a dog in the middle of the road, and I crash head-on into a parked car. Not hurt, just shaken up, I can hear the sirens blaring from somewhere behind me. I leap out of the car, manually back it up, then get back in and take off again. I'm far enough ahead of the cops that even with this lost time, I manage to continue to evade them. Or so I think, but here they are again. The chase continues. It's getting too scary! I really want to lose the cops, but I've a feeling that no matter, they're eventually going to catch up with me. Now that I no longer have to worry about Duff getting busted, maybe I can figure out a way for me to escape also. Continuing on for several more blocks, I make the turn onto Kings Highway. There's a police roadblock up ahead. Knowing this is pretty much the end of the line but not one to give up easily, I keep going. Searching for somewhere to stop the car, I think I've found the perfect spot, but when I try to stop, the brakes go out completely, and I crash head on into the "L" (the outside subway).

I've been going really fast, even faster than before. Unlike the previous crash, this time the windshield shatters into hundreds of little pieces of shrapnel, leaving me with a gashing head wound and perhaps a broken nose. With blood streaming down my face and my glasses gone, I stumble out of the car and run for a couple of blocks before I find an unbelievable hiding place. Right next to an apartment building, there's a big dipsty dumpster garbage bin in an alleyway. The whole place is pitch black, and no one can see me. I'm having a hard time catching my breath, my heart's pounding, but I'm okay, I'm safe. I can't believe how I've lucked out. It's the perfect hiding place. It's dark and the cops for sure won't find me here.

Looking out from my great hiding place, I can see and hear the cops cursing as they search for me, both on foot and in their patrol cars. Back and forth they go, searching for me with no luck. They're so upset; they can't believe they've lost me. I hear one cop yell to another, we've lost him, let's give it up. Then out of nowhere, I hear an elderly woman's voice saying, I see him officer, there he is. I can't believe it. I'm safe, home free. I've found the perfect hiding place, and then this little old lady with a strong European accent, whom I'm almost sure is Jewish, is turning me in. Doesn't she see that I'm wearing a yarmulke? The gig is up, and I feel like this blankety-blank woman, who probably is a former refugee, is turning me over to the Gestapo.

Once again, I'm under arrest. It must definitely be a great night for the men of the 67th precinct. They all appear extremely happy after the chase; you would think they captured Al Capone. The only thing that pisses them off is that my accomplice seems to have eluded them.

Cops seem to enjoy manhandling their suspects, and as I'm thrown to the ground and handcuffed, a large crowd begins to gather to see what's going on. I didn't realize before, but my face is covered in blood. Both of my hands have cuts and scratches all over them, and my back is killing me. When the paramedics arrive, one suggests taking me to the hospital, but the other guy, looking over at the cops, says no need. As they start patching me up, the cops come over to question me about my accomplice.

I tell them nothing. I don't know who the guy is, in fact I just met him tonight at some party. All I know is that his name is Joseph and he's from Queens. They know I'm feeding them a bunch of crap, but I know they're not going to do anything to me, at least not in front of all these witnesses. Since no one seems to think that I need a hospital, after the paramedic's finish patching me up, the cops put the handcuffs back on me and put me into the backseat of one of the patrol cars. We're about to pull away from the crime scene when another police car pulls up with a couple of plainclothes cops, and there's Duff sitting in the backseat. They saunter over to the car and matter-of-factly tell me that this is my accomplice and they just need my confirmation. Nope, that's definitely not him, but he does look very similar to Joseph. This guy is even wearing the same type of jacket as Joseph, but you've got the wrong guy. They're so pissed off at me, because they know I'm lying, but they've no other choice and they release Duff.

It's winter in New York and I'm freezing. Not just from the snow and rain, but I'm also soaked in sweat and now my sweat is starting to freeze. The cops pull away, and as we start the drive down to the 67th precinct, I find I'm starting to calm down. Physically, that is, but I'm really in a panic about what's about to happen to me. I've been in trouble before, arrested multiple times, but never for a real criminal act, in other words, something not political. Up until now, every time I've been arrested it was for something that had to do with the Jewish Defense League, always considered a political act. I'm now under arrest for a real criminal act, a serious felony.

In the back seat of the police car, looking out the window at the dark, snow-covered road, I'm feeling very alone. Nobody other than Duff knows that I'm under arrest, and what can he do? Like me, he's just a kid! Shit, I really messed up this time. What the hell am I going to do? At the precinct, they sit me down at a desk and remove the handcuffs. The same two detectives who detained Duff start to question me but having learnt to be a "streetwise" kid, I just keep my mouth shut except to ask to see a lawyer. Oh, I do tell them something that is an outright lie. When they ask me how old I am, I tell them I'm eighteen years old. I know if I tell the truth, they'll just call my parents. I'd probably get released, but this is not an option for me. As far as I'm concerned, my parents are no longer part of my life, and there's no way I will allow that to happen.

Fingerprinted, my pictures taken, I'm booked for various crimes and misdemeanors. The charge sheet is lengthy, some of the charges being very serious, such as grand theft auto, eluding the police, and resisting arrest. As well, there are about ten different traffic violations, the first being pretty obvious: not having a valid driver's license. In the system now, I'm just another number, both literally and figuratively. Nobody here gives a rip about me, one way or the other. I'm just another criminal booked and put through the system on any typical Saturday night in Brooklyn. After the booking procedure, I'm put into a holding cell waiting for transfer to the Brooklyn House of Detention.

In an open holding pen with about twenty thugs, I'm scared out of my mind. These guys look brutal, and the cops are just as bad because they know what goes on the moment they leave you in the cell. It's amazing how fast I've lost my bravado. Boy, do I need to get out of this mess, and fast. It will be at least a couple of more hours until they transfer us, and in a place like this, two hours can be an eternity. I'm in loads of pain and can literally feel pins and needles going through my neck and back.

When the guard comes back to place another prisoner in the cell, I tell him that I need to see someone in charge immediately. When he asks why, I tell him the truth, that I'm only fourteen years old, not feeling well, and need to see a doctor. He just laughs at me, saying it's been tried before, tell it to your lawyer. He may find it very amusing, but I don't. One of my cellmates overhears my conversation with the guard, and tells me, kid, whether or not it's true, you're still screwed. The other prisoners are going to love you when you get to the joint.

Trying to sit as far away from everyone else as possible, I'm doing my best to think, but I'm too scared. Even worse, I really need to take a piss and the only option is the one open toilet smack in the middle of the holding cage itself; I just can't.

Over the past few months, I've begun to feel and act like a big shot, even becoming a little cocky. Being in the Jewish Defense League, hanging out with mostly older kids and adults, have made me feel somewhat enlightened, more mature. I've also felt recently that even though I'm a kid, I'm so much more streetwise than the average kid. But right now, I just want to cry and go home.

It seems like forever, but finally they're moving us. The cops entering the cell handcuff and shackle all of us together. Shackled with this mean-looking guy who winks at me, I literally piss in my pants. I haven't slept all night, I'm totally exhausted, and now I'm all wet as well. We're taken down the stairs to the outside courtyard to board the prison bus, which will take us over to the Brooklyn House of Detention on Atlantic Avenue. It's snowing and still dark outside, even colder than it was when I arrived last night, and now I've more than just sweat to worry about. Two by two, we board the bus, with me sitting next to my "friend," a professional jailbird. He doesn't shut up. He just wants to share with me all that I've to look forward to once I get to the joint. Staring out the window trying to ignore him, I'm not sure, but I'm probably in shock. Continuing to look out the window, I wonder when the next time will be, or even if there will be a next time, that I'll be a free man. Never did I appreciate the dirty streets of Brooklyn as much as I do at this moment. The guard tells my seatmate to shut up, and as we drive the rest of the way in silence, I seep deeper and deeper into depression.

Arriving at the detention center, I'm ready to confess to anybody. Even ready to confess to the assassination of John F. Kennedy, if only they'll believe me. Nobody believes me or wants to believe me, and I'm learning how hard it is to change something once it's in the system. Bureaucracy's a nightmare, a lesson I'll never forget. Once you're in the system, you're stuck, with the Man preferring to send someone to prison for life rather than take on the bureaucracy. The truth is that I'm a double headache for the system. Even if they believe me, I'm still not willing to give up my parents' names and contact details. I find it amazing that although I'm in hell, I seem to be more afraid of my father than the vicious thugs I'm currently dealing with.

Thank God, the current department of corrections policy is for prisoners to be put into a private cell before their initial remand hearing. I'm put in a very small cell, one of many in a real long, dark block. My cell is stark, with just a wooden bench for sleeping and a combination sink/toilet out in the open. Hearing the cell door lock behind me, I lie down on the bare wooden bench and stare at the ceiling. I can't help it, I'm crying like a baby. I'm going to kill myself! What other choice do I have? But even committing suicide is a challenge. When I was arrested, they took away all my belongings, including my belt and even the laces from my shoes. The cell I'm in seems to be suicide proof, everything here permanently bolted down. I can't believe I'm so screwed that I don't even have the option of suicide. Moreover, it's freaking freezing in here; maybe if I'm lucky I'll freeze to death.

Cold and exhausted, I try to sleep, but the silence is deafening. After a while, one of the guards comes by, giving out old ratty blankets, and shortly after, a black cup of coffee and a bologna sandwich on white bread. Ignoring the sandwich, I drink the coffee, wondering when I'm finally going to meet with my lawyer. I've already heard from one of the jailers that even though it's Sunday, I'll have a preliminary arraignment in the morning. By law they have to provide me with a lawyer from the public defender's office, and I must get to meet with him before I go before a judge. But when? And more important, how do I convince the judge that I'm only fourteen years old?

Totally wiped out and even with this blanket, I still can't sleep. This wooden bench I'm on is hard as a rock, and with the institutional fluorescent light in the hallway that never goes out, sleep eludes me. I guess it's around five in the morning when I hear faint voices coming from down the cell block. Curious, I look out of my cell to see what's going on. At the far end of the cell block, a man in a dark suit is sitting at a small portable desk, similar to the kind of desks we had in grammar school. Facing one of the cells, he's talking with one of the prisoners through the prison bars. After about ten minutes, I see him pick up the desk, move it over to the next cell, and sit down again. Every ten minutes or so he moves again, slowly continuing down the cell block in my direction. I'm guessing he's probably the court-appointed attorney, and he's handling everyone in here who can't afford their own lawyer. That's probably almost everybody. Finally, it's my turn. When he gets down to my cell, I see what seems to be the most miserably bored, uninterested person as one could ever meet. Barely looking up at me, he starts to explain, probably for the umpteenth time that night, that he's been assigned as my lawyer from the public defender's office. Looking really young, probably just out of law school, he continues with his monologue about how he will enter a plea of not guilty on my behalf. Mumbling on, he says, then I can either post bail if I can afford it or be sent to prison until my court date. Continuing, he says, I assume you wish to plead not guilty. Either way, I'm only your attorney for this hearing, so I'm not interested in hearing your life story, just how you wish to plead.


As soon as he pauses, I immediately blurt out my whole story, babbling and crying at the same time. Mostly I tell him that I'm only fourteen years old, that I lied when I was arrested and now nobody will believe me.

I think I make his day. He actually looks up at me, as if saying, wow! Finally, something to break the monotony. For some reason, he believes me and starts asking me some probing questions. Answering all his questions truthfully, I still insist that I don't want my parents notified. That's a major challenge, he says, but he's very innovative. Is there anyone else besides your parents who can verify your age? For instance, do you have any relatives who are local? I can't believe it, he believes me. Yes, right here in Brooklyn, I say, and I give him the names and phone number of my grandparents. Nice guy as he seems, he tells me that he'll see what he can do, but I shouldn't get my hopes too high. As he explains, although I'm already painfully aware, bureaucracy is a brick wall. At this stage of the game, being that I'm already a number in the system, it might be too complicated to reverse the situation. In fact, even if we actually verify your birth date, it could still take several days to get you released. With tears still flowing down my cheeks, I ask, what's my chances? At this point, your best hope is that the judge believes that you're indeed a minor and transfers you to Juvenile Detention.

As my only hope now moves down the cell block to deal with the next "innocent" person, I find myself completely broken. It's true, I finally got someone to believe me, which means there's some hope, but it's still bad, because at the very least I'm on my way to Spofford.

Returning to the cold hard bench, I find that in spite of everything I'm breathing a little easier. I'm also beginning to relax just a little bit, thinking maybe things are going to work out after all. Although I'm still very scared, I now have some hope, which I didn't have a half hour ago. With no clock or window in my cell, I'm not sure how much time goes by, but eventually I hear the guard coming down the cell block. Opening the cell door, he orders me to my feet and puts on the handcuffs. Where's my lawyer? Definitely not interested in soothing my fears, he ignores me while shackling me to three other prisoners. We're taken through a labyrinth of hallways until we finally reach a tunnel which leads to the court annex. We're put into another holding cell, this cell unlike the previous ones, being relatively clean and airy. I'm still sweating, but now because there's heat; I'm now too hot. Where the hell is my lawyer? What's going on? Has he abandoned me? What if he forgot about me, or I go into the courtroom and there's another lawyer in his place? After all, these guys aren't like real lawyers, they're more like factory workers. They must have hundreds if not thousands of clients every month, and who am I? Maybe he was just humoring me or having fun at my expense. One by one, cases are called until finally the guard comes into the holding cell, calls my name, and escorts me into the courtroom, this time without handcuffs or shackles. Directed to the defendant's box, I wait for my turn at the docket. Looking around, I see that, thank God, my lawyer's in the courtroom, but he barely acknowledges me. As I wait for my case to be called, I look around, overwhelmed by the courtroom. It's an enormous space, with the judge sitting up high on the bench, the witness box next to him, and a stenographer in front of him taking notes. Even though it's empty right now, there's even a jury box. There are two tables set up, the prosecutor sitting at one, and at the other, my lawyer. They both have what looks like one hundred legal files in front of them. The court clerk calls my case and directs me to sit next to my lawyer. He then proceeds to read the long list of charges against me. After the reading of the charges, the judge turns and asks me if I understand the charges and if I understand my rights? I answer in the affirmative and then he asks me if I wish to enter a plea at this time of guilty or not guilty? Not knowing how to answer, I'm about to burst out in tears, when my attorney finally speaks up, asking the judge if he may approach the bench. The butterflies in my stomach are churning as my lawyer and the prosecuting attorney approach the judge and all three of them huddle in conference. After a few minutes of heated discussion, everybody returns to their normal places and the judge directs my lawyer to make his motion. My lawyer explains to the court and for the official record that I'm only fourteen years old and that my case needs to be transferred to juvenile court. He continues, explaining that he has personally spoken with my grandparents who verified my age and birthdate. Turning to me, he whispers that he told my grandparents I've been consulting with the public defender's office about some legal advice, and he just needed to confirm my birthdate.

I've always been under the impression that one needed to have been in some sort of accident for shock to set in. Right now, I feel that I'm really in shock and I seem to be having an out-of-body experience. I think I can hear the judge speaking, but everything feels so surreal. Seeming in slow motion. I think he is saying that under the circumstances the case is being transferred to juvenile court and the defendant is released on his own recognizance. I just continue to stand there looking blankly at the judge until my lawyer shakes me and says, you can go. Where? I don't understand. You're free, you can leave, you'll be notified sometime in the future about a court date in juvenile court.

I still don't understand what just happened, but the next thing I know I'm standing on the outside in the cold, right in front of the courthouse. It seems like a lifetime ago, although in reality it's less then twenty-four hours since Saturday night when I was hanging out with Duff. It's now late Sunday morning, and I'm all alone on a cold, lonely street in

Brooklyn. I'm a free man, but I no longer have a place to live; the car is gone.

**Who was that man? My entire interaction with him, all told, was probably less than thirty minutes. I was just another of hundreds of criminals and misfits who passed through his life. Probably a new lawyer just out of law school who took one of the most menial jobs a criminal lawyer can do, probably on his way up the ladder. Why would he go out of his way for me? Why not just pass me down the system? Why did he give a damn? I don't know, and I'll never know. I don't know whether this was in character, or perhaps that night he just acted differently. I don't even know his name, where he is now, or even if he's still alive. There's one thing I do know: For whatever reason, this adult took the time to care. Because of this random act of kindness he certainly saved my life, for sure virtually, but perhaps even realistically. Whoever you are, wherever you are, I thank you!**

# Chapter 16

*If you want to know who your friends are, get yourself a jail sentence.* —Charles Bukowski

By now the Man is fed up with me, and I'm fed up with the Man! The Man says I'm playing the system by being a minor, but in reality, I'm the one being played.

Although most of my crimes have been committed within the jurisdiction of the state of New York, they've a mutual arrangement with New Jersey. If a juvenile offender commits a crime in either of the two states, regardless of where the crimes themselves are actually committed, the offended state can turn over jurisdiction to the state of residence. This doesn't bode well for me, because in addition to the crimes I've actually committed, the state of New Jersey has three additional laws on its books that only a minor can be charged with: truancy, runaway, and incorrigibility. In truth I'm guilty of the first two offenses, but I'm being charged with the third, that of being incorrigible.

Even more heinous is that a juvenile has very few rights, and without even having a hearing in which I get to face my accusers, I'm sentenced to two years in a state juvenile correctional facility.

I don't even know there is a hearing. I am tried in absentia. After I'd lost my home on wheels, I'm taken in by a wonderful family in Far Rockaway. The Bieber-Feldman's welcome me with open and warm arms, treating me almost as if I were one of their own. As caring as they are, there is now an interstate warrant out for my arrest, and they have their own family's welfare to consider. So, facing some serious charges, I figure I've just two options, either keep running or turn myself in. Emotionally spent, I'm really, really beat. At just fourteen years old, I've been through hell. Spending time in and out of various schools, various jail cells, various people's basements, and of course enjoying the experience of living out of a stolen car in the dead of winter. I've no home and no security, and not just feeling very scared, I'm also feeling very vulnerable. The Bieber-Feldman's are fantastic! They are extremely kind and generous to me, but at the end of the day, I'm still not one of their own. Selma and Chaim are some of the very few adults I've been able to trust, and though I wish I could stay forever, I know I'm dreaming. To me, this is just a way station, in which I'm just passing through. Regardless of how nice they are, deep down I know that even here I'm an outsider, basically couch surfing.

New Year's Day 1976, Selma and Chaim sit me down, explaining to me the situation. We know it will be hard, but it's really in your best interest. Totally exhausted, mentally, physically, and emotionally, I just don't care anymore. I've had it, and one way or another, I just want to end this. If the Bieber-Feldman's don't want me, then what other choice do I have? I don't want to start running, spending my life always being afraid. Rather than calling the local police, Chaim speaks with my parents, arranging for them to come pick me up from Far Rockaway. Elizabeth, New Jersey is where the warrant was issued, so that's where I'll surrender to the police.

Today, January 4, 1976, which happens to be my fifteenth birthday, can really be called the first day of the rest of my life. I have butterflies flying in my stomach. Tonight my parents are coming to pick me up, with the plan of turning me over to the police. Very nervous and very scared, I'm not looking forward at all to seeing them.

All day long I've been watching the clock. I'm hanging out in the basement with Shelly and Amy, knowing that it's almost time. I'm so scared, knowing I'm about to be abandoned once again, and all three of us are crying. Mommy and Abba will be here any moment, and I'm trying to squeeze every last moment possible with these girls who've been like sisters to me. It's so hard to think about leaving.

They've arrived. I recognize my parents' voices as they're chit-chatting with Selma and Chaim upstairs. Amy comes down the stairs with two of my sisters, Chana-Szenesh and Rachel, in tow. I'm so bummed to be leaving, but I'm so happy to see them. I haven't seen them in a long time. In contrast to my parents, I get tears in my eyes when I see them and can't stop hugging them. Besides, I'm thrilled knowing that I won't be in the car alone with just my parents for the long ride back to New Jersey. Saying goodbye to these wonderful people is not easy, but I hug everybody and we're out the door. The trip to Elizabeth takes a little over an hour, pretty much the whole journey in complete silence.

It's pretty late, close to eleven p.m., when we arrive at police headquarters in Elizabeth. Everything has been prearranged, so it's a very smooth process. Two detectives from juvenile are there to meet us, immediately taking me into custody. Saying goodbye to my little sisters and ignoring my parents, I walk away, feeling once again all alone and scared.

Nothing here is personal. I'm just another juvenile offender, and it is all very matter of fact. The cops take me to be booked on the second floor, where they take my belongings away and go through the booking process. Shortly after booking is complete, these same cops handcuff me and take me for a short drive over to the Union County Juvenile Detention Center, on Broad Street.

Juvenile hall is located on the very top couple of floors of the Union County Court complex, and when we arrive, we take a special express elevator straight up to the processing center. My police escorts hand me over to the center's authorities, and I wait. It seems that everything that has to do with government authorities always takes forever. They remove the handcuffs and I once again go through another intake process, starting with a quick medical review. Told to take a shower, I'm then issued a detention center uniform, consisting of jeans, sneakers, and a shirt which has Union County Juvenile Detention Center written on it. A couple of hours of being processed, it's now about one in the morning when they finally put me into a single cell. Once again, I am alone, scared, and contemplating the future. Strangely, though, I feel a sense of security and freedom.

# Chapter 17

*Stone walls do not a prison make, Nor iron bars a cage; Minds innocent and quiet take; That for an hermitage; If I have freedom in my love And in my soul am free, Angels alone, that soar above, Enjoy such liberty.*
**—Richard Lovelace**

Unlike my past jail cells, this one has more than just the usual hard bench to sleep on. It even has a bedsheet, blanket, and pillow, but otherwise it's pretty standard, with a combination sink and toilet. A common thread of casinos and prisons, there are no windows and clocks. Intentionally kept to a minimum for psychological reasons, because they just don't want you to be able to keep track of time. Staring up at the ceiling, I'm trying to think about the future. I never really paid much attention to a ceiling before. Are those bugs or just black stains? They look like bugs, but they're not moving. It's gotta be late, nothing but deafening silence. Feeling the eerie quiet, all I'm thinking about is what's gonna happen to me. Logic tells me I'm not supposed to be happy, but in a funny way I am. Yes, I'm scared, feeling all alone, yet a certain inner peace has come over me. It's hard to explain. I feel a sense of quiet, almost like being in the womb. While I won't admit it to anyone, I'm actually loving the solitude. More and more, I'm slowly getting used to the idea that my only real friend is me, and I'm the only person that I can really depend on.

Awoken by the sounds of hustle and bustle, I know that Sunday morning has arrived. Sounds of voices, clanking, yelling, and bells are filling the air, as I nervously await to see what's gonna happen next. No matter where I am, I always have to rely on the Man, and obviously this place is the epitome of the Man. A guard opens my cell door, robotically giving me a breakfast tray, towel, and a bar of soap. When I ask some questions about what's gonna happen next, he completely ignores me. I've found that in most places like this, the guards are on such a power trip that they get their kicks by playing head games with you. Bummed, I look at my breakfast tray: a bowl of oatmeal, a couple of pieces of white bread with jelly and margarine, an orange, and a carton of milk. Looks pretty gross but I'm famished, so I devour everything.

After finishing breakfast, I'm now not just bummed but also bored. I guess I'll have to wait till lunch for my next human contact. Hot dogs with beans and potatoes, more white bread with jelly and margarine, and this time an apple. This guard is friendlier and more forthright, telling me what I need to know. He tells me that the rule is, until I'm arraigned formally, I can't be released into the general population. This means that my home at least until Monday will be this six-by-eight-foot prison cell. Breakfast, lunch, dinner, and again breakfast. It's almost like being a patient in a hospital, but here the food's lousy. Since my cell's completely self-contained, other than mealtimes, I haven't been out since my arrival on Saturday night and have barely spoken to a soul.

Monday morning is finally here. Being very tense, I haven't got much sleep since I arrived. Breakfast having been a while ago, I'm guessing it must be about midmorning when a guard finally comes to my cell, telling me to get my ass in gear because he's taking me down to the courthouse for my remand hearing. I now finally have a chance to see the layout of this place, and more importantly, I get a good look at the general population. As I'm escorted through the facility, all I can do is pray that after the hearing, they'll put me straight back into the same cell. Yes, there are no adults here, just kids, but these are not the kind of kids I want to be hanging out with.

Cocky, and once again thinking that I've so much experience in legal hearings, I expect to walk into a traditional courtroom with a judge sitting up high. But instead of a courtroom, I find myself in a large conference room, with several people in attendance. The guard sits me down next to a guy who introduces himself as my state-appointed attorney. Sitting next to him is another lawyer from the district attorney's office, a state social worker, a stenographer, and finally my mother, who is the last person I expected to see here.

It's hard to even look over at Mommy. I know it's crazy, but I feel more comfortable being with these state bureaucrats than with my own mother. Starting the ball rolling, the district attorney informs me that this is an informal predetention hearing to inform me of my rights (I have none). My sentence has already been predetermined as a minimum of two years in a state juvenile detention facility—minimum because theoretically they can keep me until I am eighteen years old. The only good news is that, in return for me being convicted of "incorrigibility," all other state and federal charges against me have been dropped.

Shit! I guess I'm slow, but it's finally starting to sink in. I'm probably going to be in this hellhole for the next two years.

Six adults in the room including my mother, but yet I feel all alone. Theoretically, because I'm a minor, each one of these people has an ethical, moral, and legal responsibility to be looking out for my best interests, but as far as I can tell, nobody here gives a damn about me. The lawyer from the district attorney's office keeps talking, and I'm sort of listening. Right now, all I can think of is that hopefully they'll just let me spend the next two years in the same cell I was just in. At least there I'll be safe. Blah, blah, blah, he continues. Hold on, what did he just say? Listening harder, I think he just said something about some other option. Yes, he's in the middle of explaining something that perks my ears. What's that? Something about a not-too-well-known government program. I hear him say that there's a number of private institutions that are contracted by the states as pseudo-detention facilities. Trying to follow, I'm confused and not really getting exactly what he's talking about. The idea behind it, he continues, is that all juvenile facilities are supposed to be in fact, rehabilitation centers rather than purely detention facilities. In reality though, it's an entirely different story. Most state-run institutions are disasters and hellholes, and most juvenile delinquents just move on to becoming delinquent adults. Knowing that the system is really hard to change, a loophole in the law was created a few years ago whereupon under certain circumstances a juvenile can be sent to one of these private places to serve out their sentence.

The Edgmead Youth Rehabilitation Center, a medium-security juvenile detention facility in Mountain Home, Idaho, is such a place. My ears perk up even more. This sounds interesting, but where the hell is Idaho? The social worker, a good-looking woman with very long, beautiful blonde hair is now doing most of the talking. She's painting a gorgeous picture of a stereotypical western ranch with horses, cows, etc., a place where I can find myself, grow, and flourish. I start to get a bit excited; this is beginning to sound really cool, although I know there's got to be a "catch," and, like anything that sounds too good to be true, there is a catch. Everybody wants in, so it's almost impossible to get a placement there, and there's an extremely long waiting list. So long in fact, that they aren't even taking any new applicants.

So, what's the point? If that's the case, why even bring it up? Is this some type of cruel joke? She continues to explain. It seems that in the few weeks prior to my arrest, my parents were working behind the scenes, hand-in-hand with the authorities. I am pleasantly surprised to learn that this time they've really stepped up to the plate.

There's the famous eighty-twenty rule. Mommy and Abba have never fit in with the 80 percent, in other words, the majority of people. Most people considered my parents to be odd, and the masses always considered them a bit of an outcast. On the other hand, the 20 percent really liked them, and because of this, they enjoyed all sorts of connections. Unbeknownst to me, when this whole situation started, Mommy and Abba took advantage of some of their connections, and with the help of Rabbi Pinchas Teitz, the community rabbi of Elizabeth, and Mr. Nilsen, they managed to secure a place for me on the Edgmead waiting list.

Of course, nothing's exactly as it seems, and there are two provisos. First and foremost, to make this all legal, I have to agree. Second, until such time as a slot opens up, which at this time is a total unknown, I will be kept incarcerated in New Jersey. My waiting time until placement will not be counted toward my actual sentence. A bit skeptical, I know it sounds too good to be true, but what other alternative do I have? Bottom line is that I've two choices: one, go along with this and hope for the best, or two, decline and spend the next couple of years in the juvenile equivalent of Attica. No brainer, I'm in.

Now that we're all in agreement, it's time to make it official. The guard escorts me across the hall into the courtroom, a real courtroom just like I've been in before. Directed to the table on the left side of the room, I sit alongside my lawyer. On the right side of the room, the district attorney, the social worker, and my mother are all seated. For the first time today, I'm now looking directly at my mother. She's staring straight ahead at the judge. I wonder where Abba is, but at least she's here. The court clerk starts by reading a whole bunch of legal mumbo jumbo. When he finishes, the judge turns to me, asking if I understand what the proceedings are about, and do I have any questions. I answer yes to the first question, no to the second. His honor continues saying, I understand that a pre-hearing agreement has been reached. Does either side have anything to add or clarify before we proceed? With no other issues at hand, his honor turns to Mommy and asks, Mrs. Freundlich, are you willing to take your son home today, until a spot opens up at the Edgmead Youth Rehabilitation Center? Looking directly at the judge, she says no, your honor, that's not possible at this time.

I'm not surprised, but it still hurts, sort of like being socked in the stomach. His honor the judge then turns to me and, along with more legal mumbo jumbo, says to me, as your mother is not willing to accept custody at this time, you are therefore remanded to the JINS detention center for a period of fourteen days. The JINS center (Juvenile in Need of Supervision) is a minimum-security temporary kiddie jail located in Berkley Heights, New Jersey. Within a couple of weeks, the inmates are either sent home or on to a permanent facility. By law, the maximum time one can be placed in JINS is fourteen days, but the loophole in the law is that this fourteen-day maximum period can be renewed repeatedly and indefinitely.

With the hearing now over, I'm back in my cell, but I don't have too much time to reflect because after a couple of hours, the guards come for me to transfer me to JINS.

# Chapter 18

*The securest place is a prison cell, but there is no liberty.*
—**Ben Franklin**

JINS is on the campus of the county mental hospital. Being a minimum security facility, JINS is for kids who have committed minor offenses, or the three "juvenile only" crimes.

Driving through the front gate and expecting the worst, I can't help but notice how beautiful the snow-covered campus is. Though it's still the middle of winter, I see that all the buildings are freshly painted a clean white, and everything looks so well maintained. As pretty as it all looks, I'm scared; after all, I'll be living in a mental institution! Mentioning my fear to the guard escorting me, he assures me that JINS is a totally separate facility that just happens to share the same campus with the mental institution, and he's right. JINS has its own separate building, with a number of facilities being shared between the residents of JINS and the mental hospital. The rule is that the residents of each institution are never ever supposed to even be in sight of one another, and although this is the case most of the time, it isn't necessarily absolute.

Once again, I'm being processed, or as known here, "intake." It feels like I'm always being processed, in one way or another, or from one place to another. JINS is a three-story building with intake on the first floor, administrative offices on the second, and the detainee residences on the top floor. JINS has a completely different feel and look to the Union County detention facility, with no bars or jail cells. The feel here is somewhere between a dormitory school and a hospital. From the central walkway, I come into a staff area that looks very similar to a nurse's station in a hospital. Adjoining the staff area, there're two dormitory wings, one for boys and one for girls. The dorm wings, each styled exactly like the other, have one long room with two sides of ten beds each. In addition, each wing has a small sitting area, toilet facilities, and a shower room. Next to the staff station, there's also a common recreation area where we get to socialize, boys and girls together.

Like every other penal institution, there are loads of rules here. One of the worst offences, along with fighting or attempted escape, is for boys to be caught in the girls' wing, or vice versa. Other than for minor infractions, immediate punishment is to be sent back to the Union County detention center indefinitely. I see that I'll be fine here. I can make this work for me, and I've no intention of screwing it up. Assigned a bed, given various personal items, and introduced to the staff, I'm once again read the riot act, in which they recite all the various rules and regulations.

I make the decision from the start that I'll continue to wear my yarmulke, but not because I'm really very observant. The truth be told, my level of observance has been dropping ever since I committed the first of my very big "no-no's." It wasn't only that I stole both the car and the cash, but I did it on the Sabbath no less. While it's pretty unusual for a kid with my background to be found in these kinds of places, the fact that I'm wearing a yarmulke really makes me stand out. When I look at myself in the mirror wearing my yarmulke, it gives me my identity. I'm not just another "loser," I'm a somebody. I've decided that I'm some sort of political prisoner.

Nobody can ever say my life is boring, but right now I can't help but feel bored out of my mind. There's nothing to do here, one day just seems to lead into the next, and nothing really exciting ever seems to happen. I'm just biding my time waiting for a slot in Edgmead to open up. In a real limbo situation, there's no end in sight. It's almost impossible to build any kind of a relationship here. Most kids are in and out within a few days, and with no kid relationships, I concentrate instead on the staff. For the most part they're really good people, and I'm starting to bond with some of the counselors, Karen in particular, who is a really nice, sweet woman who also happens to be a devout Christian. While not very religious, I'm very spiritual, and I guess because we both have a strong connection to God, it's helped create a bond between us.

With a very limited school program made up primarily of workbooks, my daily schedule is mundane. I guess because I'm such an avid reader, I'm much more advanced academically than the average resident and therefore spend most of my time helping the staff out. Who would've thought! Having hardly any formal education, going from school to school, failing every year, and I'm still light years ahead of the other residents.

My most exciting day comes every two weeks, when I get to go back to the Elizabeth courthouse for my routine remand hearing. I love it, because it's a real break in the boredom, even though it's always the same chain of events. Usually taking the entire day, I go to the same courtroom and stand before the same judge. His Honor asks the prosecution what's the status of my case and if a place in Idaho has opened up yet. The assistant district attorney always answers, no, Your Honor, not yet. The judge then turns to my mother, who's always there, asking her if she would like to take custody of me (in other words, take me home) until a slot opens up. Never looking directly at me, her answer is always, no, Your Honor, it's not possible at this time. His Honor then turns to the court reporter and says, the remand of the juvenile is extended for fourteen days to be placed at the JINS facility.

This routine goes on for about six months, repeating every two weeks. I now hold the record of the longest consecutive resident at JINS. At the intake station there's a board listing the names of all the residents, along with the number of days they've been here, and I always lead the pack.

At JINS, I'm a big fish in a small pond, and when I go to the courthouse, I'm a small fish in a big pond. But even as a small fish, pretty much everybody in this part of the courthouse knows me. It's a no-brainer that I stand out, firstly because I'm here every two weeks, but secondly, the number of yarmulke-wearing kids who pass through these walls of justice are slim to none. Everything about me stands out, even my appearance. Besides my yarmulke, I look much older than my fifteen years; in fact, I've a full beard. Also, being much more mature than the average fifteen-year-old, in combination with coming from a decent socioeconomic background, I'm definitely a rarity here. Constantly working hard on keeping my nose clean, I get along with almost all the kids, as well as the staff.

Other than my court days, most other days my main excitement is looking forward to mealtimes. We eat our meals in the hospital's staff cafeteria, walking over three times a day in a group formation. Being that I've the longest tenure, I've become leader of the pack. My unofficial promotion is not just due to my longevity but also because I'm so different, and that always seems to make me an exception to the rule. For instance, the director just announced that wearing head coverings in the dining room is no longer allowed other than for me. Why am I an exception? Because of my yarmulke. On the rare occasion when I do commit some minor infraction, my good behavior and good relations definitely help me. Almost always, the staff tend to turn a blind eye, but sometimes when my infractions aren't so minor it becomes a bit more complicated. One of those complications is Lizzie, another juvenile delinquent about my age, tall, black, and beautiful. I'm in love! Yes, I know I'm always falling in love, but there are different types of love. Besides being beautiful, Lizzie is also very bright, which is quite rare here, and we're spending as much time as we can together. It's challenging, because even though JINS is a coed facility, fraternizing between the sexes is very heavily regulated, and they're always on the lookout. There are big no-no's and little no-no's, and fraternizing is definitely a big no-no, especially getting caught in the shower room together. There are certain rules that are referred to as "no tolerance," and almost without exception is a "no tolerance" rule ever pardoned. Once again, Freddy is different, and once again, I manage to slip out of an uncomfortable situation.

I really do like most of the staff here, but I'm also smart enough to know how and when to butter them up, with the "when" being every chance I get. This particular time it's Karen who saves my butt, but it isn't the first time, nor will it be the last. New detainees come and go almost daily, and I'm oblivious to most of them. That being said, sometimes someone special crosses my path, but unfortunately, there's only one Lizzie.

One evening I'm sitting in the lounge area, minding my own business and watching television when a new detainee starts messing with me out of the blue. He starts making snide comments and cursing me, fixating on my yarmulke. I'm trying to ignore him, but he's intent on doing whatever it takes to get me riled up so I'll lose my cool. It's starting to work. I'm upset and livid, but I'm afraid to do anything in retaliation. One of the cardinal rules at JINS is that anybody who gets into a fight, regardless of who starts it, is automatically transferred to juvenile detention with no questions asked. Each day he gets bolder and bolder. He's really getting frustrated, and one night he pulls out the Hitler business, which always seems to be the failsafe for any anti-Semite. He whispers to me Hitler was right. Hearing this, I go ballistic! Definitely not thinking clearly, I get up, turn around, and pick up the oak coffee table and hurl this extremely large piece of furniture straight at his head. Lucky for him, the table just misses him, but not before breaking into a number of pieces. Boring into his eyes with a killer look, I say, if you ever open your mouth to me again, I'll take your head off. The room goes absolutely quiet. Not even the proverbial pin drops. Everyone's shocked and in no doubt about the truth in what I've just said. Within moments, the staff running in say, what's going on and who started it? The silence deafening, I wait for the inevitable. They've got closed-circuit television; there's no doubt they know exactly what's going on. This is definitely a no-tolerance rule, and they'll arrest anybody they even suspect is involved. Remembering we've no rights here and that the last word always belongs to the administration, I'm shocked when they walk away without doing anything. Two days later, this other kid is sent to juvenile detention in Elizabeth for some minor offense, and nobody bothers me again.

Two amazing lessons I learn from this incident. First, I later try to pick up just a small piece of that coffee table and I can't even budge it; it's just too heavy. Second, once you stand up to bullies, they rarely start with you again.

There's still no word about a slot opening up in Idaho. Although I'm feeling a bit more secure than I've felt in a long time, I'm still bored out of my mind. I'm a bigshot now at JINS, and within reason I've the run of the place. Much of my time is taken up daydreaming about Idaho and about how different my life will be when I finally get out there. Due to my longevity, I'm getting certain privileges that are rather unusual. One of the privileges I now have is that on the way back from my routine court hearing, I'm taken to the public library and allowed to check out books. Reading everything I can find about Idaho and the northwest United States, I find myself fantasizing about becoming a cowboy once I finally get out there.

Five months is a long time to sit around doing nothing, especially for a kid in his prime. When I came here, there was snow on the ground, and now the flowers are starting to bloom. I'm so sick of this place, really anxious to get to Idaho, but still there's no availability and nobody seems to have a clue as to when something is going to happen. Sick of it all, I make a decision: I'm getting out of this place, one way or another.

Using the payphone in the center, I call my buddy Ralph, telling him of my escape plan and asking him for help.

Although JINS is a minimum-security facility, there's still security and an alarm system, so I have to figure this out. Saturday night, right after lights out, being blessed with a roaring thunderstorm, I sneak out of bed and make my way to the fire escape chute. It is the only way out of here, other than me figuring a way of getting past security. My problem is that the alarm will start blasting the moment I'm down the chute, but I'm hoping I'll still have enough time to get away in spite of it. Opening the fire chute door, I slide down the three stories to the ground floor, and as expected the alarm starts blaring. My luck is that because this is a minimum-security facility, they aren't as quick getting their act together as they would be in a more secure facility. Before they realize what's going on, I'm already in the woods. Ralph's waiting close by with his car, and we get away with no trouble.

Always having had a challenge with instant gratification, once again I've no idea what my end game is. I know the plan is to make our way back to Far Rockaway, but then what? Having not thought this through at all, I just know that I'm sick and tired of being cooped up at JINS, and I need air! This is just an impulsive reaction to my frustration, the truth being that I've no plan and no ideas. My only idea is that I really want to get to Idaho, and I've panicked.

I get my air, but just barely. As we pull up to Ralph's house, Chaim comes running out yelling, you've got to take him back, he's on the news. It seems that through a comedy of errors there's a story on a local news program that a patient from the psychiatric hospital has escaped and that this supposed escape is affiliated with the Jewish Defense League. Pretty wild story but enough to scare the crap out of everybody affiliated with me, especially me. That being said, going back to JINS isn't as simple as it sounds. I can't just go back and say that I'm sorry and won't do it again. We do the next best thing, and Ralph drives me back to Elizabeth where I turn myself in to the cops. Booked once again, I'm transferred right back to the Union County Juvenile detention center where it all started. I'm even placed in the same cell. Amazing how things change; this time I'm not even scared, even though this will probably be my new home for a while. I guess I've toughened up, and since the rules are very simple and clear, I know that my escape will cost me. Escape is a one-time, strikeout proposition, and I'm resigned to the fact that I'm here to stay. Unusually, considering the circumstances, I sleep very well.

Monday morning I'm brought before the same juvenile court judge that I've been seeing for the past few months. I don't know what I've done to deserve this, but once again God is with me. I can't believe it when I see the director of JINS himself here in person, to ask the court to suspend my sentence. His Honor reads me the riot act but says he understands my frustration and because of that, along with my exemplary behavior record, he'll give me one more chance. He orders me to be taken back to JINS.

As luck would have it, just a few weeks later a slot at Edgmead finally opens up. After almost six months at JINS, my name is finally taken off the board, and I say goodbye to JINS.

I'm fifteen and a half years old and on my way to the Edgmead Youth Rehabilitation Center, in Mountain Home, Idaho.

# Chapter 19

*In the depth of winter, I finally learned that there was in me an invincible summer.* **—Albert Camus**

June 21, 1976, the first day of summer. Crazy to think that I've been waiting for this day for months. I'm actually excited and happy to be going off to prison. Earlier this morning a guy from social services arrived to escort me on my trip out west. Not only am I finally on my way, but I'm going to travel in an airplane; my first time ever.

As there are no direct flights to Boise from Newark, our flight takes us first to Chicago, a change of planes, and then on to Boise. Even though it's summertime, it's already dark when we finally arrive at Boise airport. Exiting the terminal, my escort turns me over to a couple of people from Edgmead who will escort me the rest of the way. Exhausted as I am after a real long day that is still far from over, I'm also very excited. All day my imagination has been on fire about the new future awaiting me. I feel sort of like those old-time immigrants from the 1800s, who were told go west young man, because that's where the opportunity is. As we drive on Interstate 85 toward Mountain Home, I'm amazed by the vastness and emptiness of the desert. Being a city boy, the difference is stark. The biggest thing that stands out for me is that there are no street lamps on the highway, and everything outside is just pitch black. I'm just lost in awe and thought. It's a long drive to Mountain Home, close to two hours, and even though they keep saying we're almost there, all I can see is darkness ahead of us. Quite suddenly, and almost out of nowhere, I see a lighted oasis smack in the middle of the desert. It seems so eerie, almost as if I'm looking at a UFO (unidentified flying object).

Wow! After months of waiting, I'm finally here, the Edgmead Youth Rehabilitation Center. As we drive past the gatehouse, down a long security road, and finally through the main gate, I see a big compound directly in front of me. It looks like a ghost town, with nobody around, just a bunch of sagebrush blowing around and a couple of dogs wandering about.

Even though it's real late, food always takes precedence, so our first stop is the main dining hall to get something to eat. After sandwiches and coffee, they take me to ICU, which is the equivalent of solitary confinement. Being that it's so late, tonight they just conduct a temporary intake, and tomorrow morning they will process me thoroughly. Unlike in other detention centers, this ICU is a dormitory with private rooms, although the one thing that makes it different is that there are bars on the windows and the doors are locked from the outside. I'm taken to room number four, which has a bed, table, chair, and all the toiletries I need. I've a million different thoughts and questions racing through my mind, but I quickly fall asleep out of sheer exhaustion.

The sun's shining through the window when a guard comes in to wake me up, only here they're called counselors. He tells me that I'll be taken to breakfast with the rest of the ICU inmates, who eat their meals separately from the general population. Walking out of ICU, the first thing I notice is the heat. Even though it's still early, I discover quickly that desert weather is very different from east coast weather. Even in the summer, nights can get extremely cold, and the days are always wickedly hot. In formation of two by two, we're escorted to the dining room, and I'm now able to check out the place. In contrast to last night, the place is bustling with people. I'm checking them out and they're checking me out, but all I really notice is the stares I'm getting. Obviously, the stares are because I'm the new kid on the block, but I assume what's really making me stick out like a sore thumb is my yarmulke. I'm willing to bet most of these kids don't even know what a yarmulke is.

After breakfast, it's off to the administration wing where my intake really starts. After first going through all the routine stuff, which I've done numerous times before, I'm taken to the infirmary for a thorough physical exam.

After lunch, I'm scheduled to meet with the director of Edgmead, the caseworker assigned to me, and the senior counselor from the unit I'm being assigned to.

Bill Coons, the director, seems to be a pretty nice guy but a bit of an oddball. He does most of the talking, explaining all the rules, what I can expect, and what is expected of me. While Mr. Coons may be a nice guy, my case worker, Humphrey Richardson, turns out to be a real jerk. One of the first things he does is to convince me that it wouldn't be in my best interest to continue wearing my yarmulke. I can't say in full conscience he threatened me, but he got his point across and I acquiesced.

After finishing with these guys, John takes over. John is my senior unit counselor and seems to be a tough but decent guy. Pulling no punches, he explains to me how the law works at Edgmead, from the worst possible punishment to the best possible scenario. The worst possible scenario being that I really screw up and they send me back to New Jersey to complete my sentence in a real detention center. For that to happen, I would have to do some real serious crimes, not what are referred to here as infractions. Edgmead has a carrot-and-stick approach, which is a five-tier justice system called the "form" system. Form 1 being the highest, in terms of having the most privileges, and Form 5 being the lowest. We're not inmates or detainees here, but residents, and as a new resident, I enter at a Form 4, which gives me very few privileges. Every week there's a staff meeting during which a review of all the residents is done, and every resident has a right to submit a petition asking for anything, from a special privilege, furlough, appeal of a sentence, or most of all an upgrade to the next form level. If your behavior warrants it, your petition is accepted and you go up a form, which gains you more privileges. You can only go up a maximum of one form per week, and of course if you break any of the rules you're demoted, with there being no maximum number of forms you can drop. A very serious infraction such as attempted escape, fighting, stealing, etc. would automatically send you to ICU for whatever amount of time they feel like punishing you with, plus an automatic drop to Form 5, which leaves you with no privileges.

Like JINS, Edgmead is a coeducational facility, and like JINS, there are no prison uniforms; we can wear whatever we want. I'm assigned to unit two, which is one of twelve units, half for girls and half for boys. Each unit, fashioned after World War II–type barracks, has a maximum capacity of twenty-four residents. There are two long lines of beds in each unit along with a small kitchenette, television room, and bathroom with shower facilities. Each unit has a senior counselor and three assistant counselors on each eight-hour shift. Much of the logistics here is similar to what I'm used to from my other institutional stays, but because this is a rehabilitation center, the terminology and focus are very different, which will take time getting used to. It really doesn't matter what they call these places, because what makes them all the same is the power that the Man has over you.

Every institution I've ever been in, including the various schools, has their official and unofficial rules. Penal institutions also have their official and unofficial rules, the difference being that the inmates also have their own set of rules, and I'm expected to know them all. Ignorance of the law is not considered a valid excuse, with anyone. The main rule here, as in every other correctional facility, is that the staff is always right and never, ever question that rule.

Being the new kid on the block, my mission first and foremost is to keep my head down, learn the system, and keep my nose clean. Part of the system is that whenever someone new arrives at an institution of any kind, there's always going to be a power play. Everybody wants to know who I am, what my story is, and where I stand on all sorts of stuff. Unbeknownst to me I've already arrived with a solid reputation. There are very few secrets in these types of places, and I'm already a "known," and an "unknown," both at the same time.

My "known" is that I'm involved with the Jewish Defense League, which makes me a cross between a terrorist, a political prisoner, and a mafia type of guy, and my "unknown" is exactly the same. I'm an anomaly. Neither the residents nor staff at Edgmead have ever come across someone quite like me before. Edgmead, basically a white-collar kiddie prison, has seen plenty of residents with socioeconomic backgrounds similar to mine, from time to time even Jewish kids, but there's never been someone quite out of the box like me. As a professional institutional resident, I'm very aware of my strengths and weaknesses, and I've learnt how to play the game. Over the past couple of years, I've become somewhat of an expert at hiding my true feelings, because true feelings can bring big trouble, even sometimes get you killed. This is not the first time I've been really scared, but I now know how not to show it.

Rumors abound. There are all sorts of stories circulating about me, some true, others not. Regardless, every chance I get, I exaggerate and enhance the stories. As in most similar places, you'll find groups that either are real gangs or more just a group. While there are no real gangs here, we have groups of kids who hang together, calling themselves "clubs." Most people, whether they're kids or adults, whether they're prisoners or not, need a sense of belonging, and Edgmead is no different. The difference in a place like this is that belonging also buys you protection.

It's never very pleasant to be a lone wolf because it makes you vulnerable. Once again, I'm the exception to the rule. I'm both a lone wolf and not a lone wolf; again, I'm an anomaly. Pretty much getting along with everybody, staff and residents alike, I avoid most problems, but this involves a lot of hard work. In any penal institution, whether for adults or kids, much of life revolves around staying in one piece, both physically and mentally. Part of the secret to my success is being friendly with everybody, but not too friendly. I intentionally have to remain some sort of a mystery, partially because it feeds my ego, but more importantly, I have to be wary of those who might give me trouble, and there's always someone out there who's looking for trouble. Always having to be on my toes, I'm constantly reminded of my father who would say, you have no real friends, just playmates, schoolmates, cellmates, etc. Right now, I don't have any friends, just mates.

# Chapter 20

*Every man can transform the world from one of monotony
and drabness to one of excitement and adventure.*
## —Irving Wallace

Edgmead being a rehabilitation center, education is supposed to be a really big deal, and a major part of the day-to-day curriculum. Being here is meant to take away any more excuses I may have for not getting an education. After all, the teachers here are supposed to be experts in dealing with kids like me, although right now, it's not my worry. Summer's arrived, and with the school year pretty much over, I don't have to worry about school until September.

Edgmead is located about five miles outside the city limits of Mountain Home, a small town of fewer than six thousand people. The two main industries here are Edgmead and the Mountain Home Air Force base, which is located on the other side of the city. Most of the townspeople have practically nothing to do with Edgmead, and because Edgmead is a secure facility, there are lots of rumors in town about the goings-on here. The "campus," as it's known, is U-shaped with about thirty buildings. Each building looks the same from the outside, all prefabricated metallic green. From the inside of the compound, the architectural design is created in such a way that you don't know you're in prison. In fact, the perimeter fence is placed so far back, it gives the place a pretty good feel, and sometimes I even forget where I am. That feeling is always short lived, though, because regardless of physical appearance, we're constantly reminded of where we are, in one form or another.

Almost a military type of existence, we're told where to go, when to go, and how to go. It could be much worse though, and if you play by the rules, life isn't so bad, especially considering the alternatives. Playing by the rules isn't always so easy, because many times it's hard to know what the rules are. There are rules for everything, from when to get up in the morning until lights out at night. Wake up is at 06:30. We have thirty minutes to do our business, make our beds, and get ready for inspection. Failing inspection or any other infraction gives you at least a demerit. Three demerits in one week is an automatic drop in form. We also march everywhere in formation, to meals, classes, and pretty much everywhere. To go anywhere by ourselves, we have to ask for special permission, whether it's to the infirmary, going back to the unit because we forgot something, or any other possible venue.

The rules are complicated, because there are different rules for different people, all depending on one's form level. Forms 1 and 2 rarely have to be in formation, but you still have to be everywhere by the prescribed time, or you get a demerit. With much more freedom, you don't have to ask permission for every little thing.

Even in the summer, they keep us busy with various educational and recreational activities, in which rehabilitation is always at the forefront. They keep drilling into us that the purpose of our incarceration is to turn us into productive members of society. With all these activities, three meals a day, and all sorts of therapy sessions, we're pretty wiped out by the time lights-out comes at 10:30 p.m. On weekends there's a different schedule with a bit more free time, but even our free time is highly structured and regulated.

The recreational facilities on campus include a recreation hall, library, swimming pool, gymnasium, and my favorite, the working farm. There are cows, horses, sheep, goats, and smaller animals. Part of our rehabilitation is working and taking care of the animals, which is a novel experience for me. While many of my fellow residents detest working with the animals, I love it, finding it very soothing. Really in love with the horses, almost every day I try to go horseback riding.

The most minor thing can result in a demerit, loss of form, or even worse. During these first ninety days, I'm learning the system and trying to get a good feel for the place. While my original dreams about coming out west haven't materialized exactly as I'd imagined, it does look like at the very least, I'll learn to ride a horse like a cowboy.

In the recreation hall, which is co-ed, there's of course a television, along with pool tables, ping-pong tables, and lots of other types of games. Because it's one of the few places that both boys and girls can fraternize legally, we spend a lot of our free time here. We also have a television in every unit's sitting room, but girls are never allowed in the boys' units, and vice versa.

Every day, as I become better acclimated, I also find that I'm becoming more ingrained into the system. This of course has not happened in a vacuum; I've been working very hard on keeping my nose clean. Not always easy, as many times there's other parties involved who can, and sometimes want to, pull you down. My biggest personal challenge is my temper, and I'm very sensitive to even the slightest slur about being Jewish. While I spent the earlier part of my childhood running, here I have to keep myself in check. This is especially true when it comes to fighting, which as in every place is one of the most serious crimes. It doesn't matter who starts it, both parties are in trouble, which means automatic ICU and form five. Trouble is something I prefer to avoid, for a couple of reasons. First, I value my lifestyle too much. Second is that I have a reputation to maintain. In life a reputation is everything, but in prison it can make the difference between life and death. My reputation here is based on innuendos and rumors, some of which preceded me and others I've embellished. Nobody, including the staff, really understands what I'm totally about; they just know I'm not the normal resident they're used to. My uniqueness gives me a bit of a wow, which I use to my advantage every chance I get. As in JINS, I've established good relations with most of the staff, with a couple becoming rather close, and, keeping my nose clean, I'm now master of my domain, reaching Form 1.

One of the most important life lessons I'm learning here is that if you want something, just ask for it. At worst the answer will be no, but if you don't ask then it's definitely a no. We're encouraged to ask for anything we want, no matter how absurd it may sound. We get to do this through a weekly petition system, in which petitions are submitted through administrative hearings. If someone tries to abuse the system or sends up a frivolous petition, they'll lose their petition privileges for a certain amount of time, but all in all, the system is pretty fair.

Although it seems like I've been at Edgmead for years, it's only been about three months since I first arrived, and all in all, my life's pretty good. I've had my ups and downs, good days and bad days, but today I'm feeling great. I've just reached the highest possible level of privileges at Edgmead; Form 1H, the H standing for honor. Form 1H is when a resident has not only reached Form 1, which in itself is a big deal, but has kept the status for six consecutive weeks. Being that becoming a Form 1 is so hard to get in the first place, reaching Form 1H has made my ego swell. If I wasn't before, I'm now really a big man on campus.

Form 1H is an enviable status, with various extra privileges besides even the special ones that Form 1s are normally entitled to. Probably the most special of these extra privileges is a pass to go into Mountain Home alone on Saturday night. Reaching this level is the equivalent in other institutions to being a trustee. I may be in prison, but not only is everything going well for me, after just a short while, I'm already pretty much running my own show. As long as I keep my nose clean, all will remain good.

One of my tricks to keeping my nose clean is trying to be friendly with everybody while in fact having no real close relationships. Being that I'm so different, avoiding intimate relationships isn't that difficult when it comes to boys, but girls are another story. Exciting things are beginning to happen to me regarding the opposite sex. Since I left my "normal" world behind, and especially after having been to Camp Jedel, girls more and more seem to notice me. It's both exciting and flattering when girls want to get close to me. Just like in JINS, getting too close to girls is a major no-no, but there are always ways to get what you want, especially if there's a "will." Being free to go into town by myself for a few hours each week makes my "will" that much easier.

Being king of the mountain feels great, but like everything else in life it can be a double-edged sword. One of the biggest challenges to being on top is that there's always somebody who wants to pull you down, and that means I always have to be on my guard.

# Chapter 21

*When you see someone putting on his Big Boots, you can be pretty sure that an Adventure is going to happen*

## . —A.A. Milne

When I first arrived, I felt I finally had some firm ground under my feet, even though it meant incarceration. Knowing where I'd be for the considerable future, no longer scared and running, I resigned myself to the inevitable. Now, after three months here, I'm actually having some kid fun. All things considered, my current situation is pretty darn good. Considering the fact that at the end of the day, I'm in a penal institution, life's not so bad. I'm respected, have no real worries, and even have a girlfriend! Stacy's a "wow," and even though this can get me into big trouble, I don't care. I'd never imagined that just maintaining a relationship with a girl could be so fraught with danger, but it's a risk I'm willing to take. What's the logic of the Man? Why do they set us up like this? They know very well that putting young boys and girls together is a recipe for trouble.

But leave it to Freddy to screw it up! I've always had a strange need for action, even to my detriment. It seems that if I'm not under some sort of stress, I start getting depressed. Worrying that something stressful is about to happen, I fulfill my own prophecy, and something then happens. I guess this is what addiction's about. Whether happy or sad, one has an almost magnetic pull to whatever it is they're addicted to. Some people are addicted to alcohol, drugs, or even food. Me, I'm addicted to action! One of the perks of being a 1H is that we're periodically taken on trips. One's scheduled at the end of summer, for Yellowstone National Park, which is located mostly in Wyoming although the park also spreads into parts of Montana and Idaho. Mr. Coons has an old used Greyhound bus, and as a hobby had turned it into a motor home. So, Mr. Coons, one supervisor, and five of us honor residents set out for Yellowstone Park in an Edgmead van and Mr. Coons's bus. One of the most exciting trips of my childhood! For one whole week we get to see some of the most beautiful scenery that God created. I never realized there was so much beauty in nature. The wildlife we observe is out of this world. Up close, big and small, we see all kinds of animals: bison, bears, bighorn sheep, and bobcats. Elk, mule deer, and white-tailed deer, moose, mountain lions, and goats, plus lots of smaller animals like wolves and foxes. I never even knew what a geyser was, let alone that Old Faithful, the geyser that Yellowstone is famous for, can shoot water as high as 190 feet into the air. Seeing and learning things that I never even knew existed, I have a fabulous trip. Camping most of the time, we set up our tents right next to Yellowstone Lake, where we fish and swim almost every day. Each morning, we wake up to the sounds and smell of bacon, eggs, and fried potatoes sizzling on the campfire. Dinner, we have amongst other things, fresh trout that we caught ourselves, along with great campfires, roasting marshmallows, and hot dogs. Our campsite is close to some of the best hiking trails in Grand Teton National Park, and every day we either go on a hike or tour around the area.

We're free to roam in some of the nearby towns, and one day the five of us kids, the cream of the crop at Edgmead, all 1Hs, hang out in town, mostly window shopping. Even though we all should be in a real prison, we've absolutely no real worries and are in fact just enjoying the life of Riley. Yet that's not enough for us. We decide we need action. Walking into a souvenir shop we decide to shoplift some items but thank God we aren't caught.

What the hell was I thinking? For some stupid two-bit souvenirs, I risked blowing it all. I had risked throwing everything I'd achieved straight into the dustbin. Why the hell did I do it? Maybe low self-esteem, maybe I felt everything was going too well, or maybe I just succumbed to peer pressure. It could be any number of reasons or a combination, but maybe I just needed an adrenaline run.

Having escaped that potential catastrophe, our great week is over and it's time to return to Mountain Home. Not only has the trip ended, but along with it the summer, meaning now the school year is officially starting. Deciding to buckle down, I'm up against the same challenge I had in JINS. Even though I think I'm not educated, after testing me, they find that I'm way above average. Most of the kids here barely having basic writing, reading, and arithmetic skills, so instead of me learning, I now find myself helping the teachers in the classroom.

Along with the new school year starting, a new resident arrives. Also from New Jersey, Pete's no amateur. He's a serious thief, specializing in automobile and home burglaries. Like me, Pete comes from the right side of the tracks. In fact, he comes from a really wealthy family in Morristown with lots of serious political connections. A guy like him really should have been sent to a maximum-security facility, but his family is so well connected politically that they cut him a deal, sending him to Edgmead. Pete's unlike any other kid I've met here, and we immediately hit it off, quickly becoming friends. He's a great guy, really funny, and we have loads of fun together. Pete's a very smart guy with lots of skills that I admire, some of them legal, but most of them not so legal. Spending a lot of time picking each other's brain, we enjoy teaching each other our mutual skills.

One of the skills I excel in is manipulating the system, specifically arranging things in my favor. Doing this every chance I get means that I'm constantly petitioning the administration for one request or another. One of the areas constantly on my mind is my Jewish heritage. While I stopped being observant a while ago and haven't worn my yarmulke since I arrived, from a nationalistic point of view, I'm just getting stronger all the time. My Jewish pride being very important to me, I make sure that everyone knows it. It's not just about nationality; it seems to give me my purpose for life. All very well and good, but it means a constant headbutt with my caseworker. Humphrey thinks he can snuff it out of me, but he's no idea how powerful a part of me it is. I won't let him intimidate me. Whether it means maintaining certain dietary restrictions or trying to observe the holidays, I'm always doing my utmost to keep my Jewishness at the forefront of my life.

The State of Idaho is currently one of only two states in the entire country that doesn't have a real organized Jewish community. This is ironic, because Idaho actually had a sizable Jewish community in the nineteenth century and also was the first state west of the Mississippi to have a Jewish governor. Here in the seventies, though, there's only one synagogue in the entire state, located in the state capital, Boise. Congregation Ahavath Israel only holds services on the Jewish high holy days and on some other special occasions. I petition the forms committee for special permission to attend synagogue services on the Rosh Hashana holiday and am pleasantly surprised when they grant my request.

Rosh Hashana in Boise is a real treat, and I'm really looking forward to going back for Yom Kippur, which is coming up in about ten days. Not expecting any blowback, I once again petition the administration for permission to attend. Not having any reason to be concerned, I sleep well. After all, nothing's changed, I'm still a form 1H.

It's the usual Wednesday administrative meeting, and after submitting my petition for Yom Kippur, I just sit back and wait. To my utter shock, my request is denied. I can't understand what's going on. I'm the perfect resident. I never make trouble. Not only that, I was also on my best behavior for the Rosh Hashana holiday, so, what's the problem? I've got to find out what's going on. Investigating, and knowing I've done nothing to deserve the rejection, I find out that everyone voted in my favor with the exception of my nemesis, Humphrey, who vetoed it. What a jerk! From the very beginning of my incarceration here, starting with the removal of my yarmulke, he's had a problem with me. Humphrey's not only my caseworker but also a psychologist I have to meet with once a week. He feels that too much Jewish exposure will be somehow detrimental to my rehabilitation. Shocked, I appeal, but he's probably not going to budge, so I'm not surprised when again I'm denied. It seems Humphrey is always trying to deflate my enthusiasm for Judaism and

Jewish causes. Even though my appeal is denied, they suggest that perhaps as an alternative, I could go to the local Mountain Home Air Force base, which they understand is holding Yom Kippur services. I don't get it. I understand that being able to attend outside services anywhere is an extra privilege not usually available to residents, but I don't understand why even though I'm a Form 1H, Boise is out but somehow the air force base is okay.

I'm pissed. I don't get it, but I'm resigned to it. Maybe I'll actually enjoy it. Up till now, I've just heard about the base but never been there. In fact, I don't think I've ever been on a real active military base before. Always a dreamer, I start to get really excited, spending most of my time fantasizing about my upcoming trip to the air force base.

A couple of days before Yom Kippur, I find myself involved in a small altercation with another resident. As Murphy's Law would have it, Humphrey witnesses the scene and immediately demotes me down to a Form 2. This is such an unbelievably minor incident that usually would be overlooked, especially with both of us swearing that we were just playing around. Nonetheless, Humphry the jerk is not going to let it slide, insisting I be demoted with no chance of appeal. Of course, in addition, the real casualty is that I can't go to the air force base for Yom Kippur. I'm livid. Humphry is a son of a bitch and probably an anti-Semite to boot. I want to kill him!

Pete is nearby, and I'm lucky he is because he's one of the few who is capable of calming me down. Once I'm calmed but still in a really foul mood, Pete has the answer for me: escape! Since I've known Pete, he's always wanted out and always wanted me to go with him. Now he thinks I'm ripe. I'm livid, not thinking straight, and he knows it. Pete knows which buttons to press. He knows me well enough by now to know where I'm vulnerable. It's not too hard for him to convince me to go over the wall.

I still try to appeal Humphrey's decision, and even though the majority is in my corner, Humphrey has veto power in this case. It's late Friday afternoon when I get the final bad news, and Pete wastes no time on working on me. By Saturday evening he's convinced me, but even though I agree, I'm sure we're not going anywhere. I'm probably just having an emotional release, knowing in my heart that I want to run away, but also knowing that it's not really feasible. First and foremost, we haven't done any planning, so other than letting off steam, I'm really not going anywhere. What I'm not aware of is how ready Pete is. He's been planning this for quite some time, just waiting for the right moment and the right partner to come along. He's probably been planning this from the first moment we met. Although he always wanted to escape with me, he probably would've gone with almost anybody, but as they say, timing is everything. For me it's the right time and the right place, and I'm ready, willing, and able.

# Chapter 22

*Genius is one percent inspiration and ninety nine percent perspiration.* —Thomas Edison

The most complex and thoroughly thought-out crimes are often successful or not due to just plain dumb luck. Sunday night, which appropriately enough also happens to be Yom Kippur, and we're ready for our big escape! No moon and a powerful storm; talk about great luck. Pete is a little older than me, seventeen, and this is his show. He has the expertise and done the planning. I'm just following his lead. Right after lights out and bed check, we grab our things and climb out the bathroom window heading for the motor pool. Torrential rains are coming down, with loud thunder and lightning, keeping everyone indoors. Nothing's stirring. Not even the cats and dogs. Nobody sees us as we make our way between the buildings. Pete quickly and quietly scans the parking lot until he spots the car he's already staked out: a facility station wagon that somehow Pete knows has a full tank of gas. Quickly picking the lock, we climb in and he hotwires the vehicle and slowly starts driving toward the front gate. We're determined to get out of the compound as quickly and efficiently as possible.

We quickly realize that the windshield wipers aren't working. Definitely can be a serious challenge on a night like this, but it ends up turning into a big advantage. With no moon out and it being completely dark, we drive up to the front gatehouse. The guard, who has no reason to suspect that we're anybody other than who we're supposed to be, waves us right through. I'm freaking out, sure that any minute we will be hearing sirens and alarms and seeing spotlights. One moment passes, then two, five, ten, twenty...nothing happens. We continue calmly driving down the road with Pete making sure not to go over the speed limit. Because the windshield wipers aren't working, in addition to me being the navigator,

I have to constantly climb out of the passenger window to wipe the excess rain off the windshield.

After about an hour on the road, we start to relax a little, realizing that up till now everything has gone in our favor. Thank God the radio works, so with map in hand and Pete driving, we listen to Led Zeppelin singing, "Stairway to Heaven."

Taking turns driving, we make sure only to use back roads. These rural roads are dark and very lonely, but we want to be as cautious as possible. Avoiding the main highways, three hours later we cross the state line into Nevada. Driving across the border from the desert of Idaho to the desert of Nevada, we let out a whoop; we now feel free! We're on a real high, even though we still don't know exactly where we're going or exactly what we're going to do once we get there, but we don't care because we already feel like we made it. You would think being surrounded by the desert in Mountain Home we'd already be experts on the desert, but somehow the Nevada desert seems different, never ending. Our adrenaline has not stopped racing from the moment we made our escape from Edgmead last night. With our emotions and hormones flowing like racehorses, we keep going. We're in shock that we even made it through the night, but now that the sun is starting to come up, we're really on a high with the smell of freedom.

Knowing that we're somewhere in Nevada but otherwise not having a clue as to where we are, we start to get a little concerned. To complicate matters, the car runs out of gas, coming to a standstill on the side of the road, leaving us somewhere in the middle of the desert with not a soul in sight. The sun is rising over the horizon, and we're already starting to feel the heat. We know from our Idaho experience that it'll just get hotter and hotter as the day progresses. Personally not good with heat, my imagination is already feeling it. Pete and I are city boys and we know how to survive in an urban environment, but not in the wild. We've no food or water, and our euphoria is starting to wind down as reality sets in. As I take in the surroundings, I see nothing but vast emptiness. There is absolutely nothing in any direction other than sagebrush, and then it hits me: We're totally out of our element. Not only are we out of both food and water, Pete is as clueless as I am. Figuring the best thing we can do is to just sit and wait it out, we hope that eventually someone will happen along. By the looks of it, this seems to be a real road, which means that sooner or later someone has to come along, right? Hopefully we'll then be able to catch a ride to the nearest town. The big question on our minds is whether it will be sooner or later. Not even midmorning yet, the temperature is soaring. As the temperature rises, so do our nerves. The minutes turn into hours, the sun is growing even stronger, and as the hours go by, I start to wonder about the wisdom of this whole idea. Life wasn't really so bad at Edgmead; so what if Humphrey is a big fat jerk. In the big picture I was winning. Wow, I get it now: He played me. He wanted me to fail, knowing exactly which buttons to push to get me to screw up.

What a valuable lesson, one that I hope I remember. I need to be proactive not reactive. I let Humphrey dictate my life when I didn't have to. I really screwed up, but I've learned a valuable lesson. Success is the best revenge, and someday I'm going to show him.

Around high noon, as best as we can figure, we finally see a car coming down the road. Hot, sweaty, hungry, and thirsty, the last thing we think about is civilities and politeness. Not being subtle at all, we don't stick out our thumbs and politely hope they'll stop. We stand in the middle of the road waving the driver down, at the same time praying they'll indeed stop. I know that we've got to be looking a little bit weird, and to tell the truth, if I was the driver of that car, the last thing I'd do is stop. Thank God I'm not the driver, because they pull over. I must be seeing a mirage, because what I think I'm seeing are two of the most beautiful women I could ever imagine getting out of the car.

Beautiful yes, mirage no. We tell them that we're on a road trip from Idaho, heading toward Las Vegas, and we ran out of gas. Would they please give us a ride to the nearest town where we can pick up some gas? Our story to them is that once we get the gas, we'll find a ride back to pick up the car. The truth is that we hope never to see that car again. In fact, we need to put as much distance as we can between us and the car before it's discovered.

Amy and Jackie are unbelievable! They're as nice as they are beautiful and tell us that the nearest town is over an hour away. As we drive, they share that they're working girls (prostitutes) who work on a fancy ranch a couple of hours from Reno, Nevada. Unlike in any other place I've ever heard about, it seems that under certain conditions prostitution is legal in some parts of Nevada. The girls are extremely friendly, sharing with us all about their stories, about where they are originally from, how much they enjoy working at the ranch, and so on and so forth. Amy explains that they were hanging out in Los Angeles for a few days' vacation, and now they're on the way back to the ranch. We feel so comfortable in their presence that Pete tells them the truth, the whole truth about everything, including how old we really are. I'm a bit scared because I figure this isn't going to end well and that we're probably on our way to the nearest sheriff's station, but they don't flinch. Instead, they're really cool, and they invite us to stay with them at the ranch. I must either be hallucinating or have died and gone to heaven. With no better options, we take them up on their most gracious offer and head for the ranch.

So much of my knowledge comes from books and films. When we pull up to the ranch, all I can think is that this place is pure Hollywood. As we drive up the long driveway and reach the main house, again I feel just like in a movie. The house has a long front porch with several white, comfortable-looking rocking chairs with small tables next to them. Parking the car, the girls tell us to make ourselves comfortable on the porch. Order anything you want, it's on our tab, just make sure it's nonalcoholic. They add, we'll be back shortly, we need to go talk to the boss. Pete and I are in a complete daze, unable to believe this is really happening. We're both sure this must be a dream and we're going to wake up any minute in a jail cell, but then again, how can we both be having the same dream? A very friendly plump black woman comes out of the house (again, just like in the movies) and serves us the most delicious lemonade I've ever tasted, along with sandwiches. You boys want anything else, she asks? No thanks. The moment she's gone, we ravish the sandwiches. We haven't eaten in close to twenty-four hours and we're famished. The sandwich is my favorite; tuna fish salad on rye bread with lettuce, tomato, and a side of coleslaw. Even here in the middle of the Nevada desert, they know to throw in a kosher pickle. I'm in heaven. My stomach is full and now I'm just going to relax.

Just chilling in the rockers, Pete sipping his lemonade, we look at each other without saying a word, praying that this moment will never end.
I don't know how long I've been dozing, but it feels really good. I haven't felt this relaxed in a long time, so when the girls return with their manager, I'm not sure if I'm still dreaming. Without saying much, he just introduces himself to us and says enjoy your stay. I don't know exactly what the girls told him, and I don't think it was the whole truth, but who cares. The bottom line is that both Pete and I feel like we've just hit the jackpot. Our new best friends Amy and Jackie escort us to our room in an adjacent building. This is not your normal hotel room, it's a suite and like something out of the movies. I've never experienced anything like this in my life. This is a real wow. The motif is Old West, but authentic Old West. I feel as if we've gone back in time a hundred years and in style. We have free run of the place but with one caveat: The main building is off limits after six in the evening.

I'm in heaven; certainly not the heaven my rabbis in elementary school taught me about, but in my mind, heaven couldn't be any better. Amy and Jackie are angels who're treating us like their little brothers. In all honesty, I can't really say we're looking at them as if they're our sisters, but either way I'm in love.

For five days, we just chill out. I know this is wishful thinking, but I can't help but keep praying that somehow we can stay here forever. Unfortunately, after almost a week, the girls tell us that it's time for us to move on, and we start making plans to move out of this fantastic bubble.

Angels come in all shapes and sizes, sometimes coming from out of nowhere. Amy and Jackie are true angels who as far as I'm concerned have earned their ticket straight to heaven. As if everything they have done for us isn't already enough, they give us a ride down to the bus station, and as their last act of kindness they give us some cash for the bus, plus a bit extra.

# Chapter 23

*Man makes plans and God laughs.* —Old Yiddish proverb

Not having a lot of money in our kitty, even with the cash the girls gave us, we figure the smartest thing to do is not take the bus but hitchhike instead. Even though we told the girls that we were heading toward Las Vegas, the truth is that our plan from the very beginning was to head back to the East Coast where we both had connections. The plan got diverted when deciding that our first priority was getting out of the state. We headed for Nevada because it was the closest state border, but now we're farther west than we'd imagined. Since we're already on our way, we decide instead to change destination and find our way to Los Angeles. Our reasoning is that even though I don't personally know any of them, if we can somehow get to Los Angeles, I can get hold of some JDL contacts, figuring they'll help us make our way back to the East Coast. Normal stupid kids, we're so naïve. We think we know it all, but in truth we're a total mess. Regardless, and through it all, no matter what stupid things I do, it always seems that the one above keeps me out of harm's way.

It's getting late in the day and already starting to get dark. This means it's also starting to get cold and we're frustrated because we have been out here for hours trying to catch a ride. Suddenly, a blacked-out van stops with a couple of guys in it, who ask us where we're headed. Los Angeles, we answer. Great, that's exactly where we're headed, but before we can get into their vehicle, they add the caveat that nobody rides for free; cash, grass, or ass. We decline because we don't have much of the first, none of the second, and are not willing to provide the third. Bummer, because we really needed this ride, but it always seems to work out for us in the end, and shortly afterward we catch a free ride. I don't know why God loves me so much, but about one hour later, we happen to pass that same blacked-out van, where we get the pleasure of witnessing them being handcuffed and put into a state patrol cruiser.

It's slow going, but we continue on our journey, ride to ride, some for short hauls and some for longer. Throughout, we meet loads of mostly interesting people. Sometimes they're jerks, but for the most part, they're good people who just want to be of service. Some days we're treated to food, sometimes we live off the land, and sometimes when we have no choice, we dip into our small stash of cash to buy stuff. Sleeping wherever we can find a place, one night we're on a park bench, the next night in a barn or a haystack. (By the way, sleeping in a haystack is not like the movies; it's extremely uncomfortable.)

One evening, feeling desperate and stuck at a truck stop where we've been trying for hours to catch a ride in the right direction, we're drinking coffee and looking out the window. We notice a couple of guys who look "cool." Which direction are they headed? San Francisco. Can we catch a ride? Sure, welcome aboard! No longer headed to Los Angeles but to San Francisco. The two cities are pretty much on the opposite ends of the state, and about an eight-hour drive from one end to the other. Being that we're clueless, to us California is California, and we graciously accept the ride. Climbing into their van, we see very quickly that these guys are the polar opposite of those two other jerks who ended up being busted for who knows what. In fact, these guys are so nice that they're willing to share their "grass, cash, and ass" with us. Unlike Pete, I respectfully decline most of their generous hospitality.

When we finally arrive in San Francisco later that night, they ask us if we've a place to stay. We of course don't and we accept their gracious offer of their place to spend the night. I call it unbelievable hospitality. Nowadays it's what they call couch surfing, but either way, for me it's another example of the very unusual kindness of a stranger. The next morning, awakened by the sunlight flowing in through a big beautiful bay window, I'm amazed to see the Golden Gate Bridge. For a moment, I can't remember where I am, nor how I got here. Looking around, all I can see from one side of the room to the other is that it's overflowing with various flowers and plants, most of them marijuana plants. Hearing voices coming from the kitchen, it seems that everybody else in the house is up, so after quickly getting up, I realize I haven't taken a shower in who knows how long. Great shower, followed by a great breakfast of eggs, toast, and coffee, then we say a million thanks and good-bye.

With time having lost some of its meaning, Pete and I head to a nearby park to figure out our next move. We've been on the run now for close to two weeks, and now that we're in San Francisco, we congratulate ourselves on a successful escape. I figure the chances of us getting caught now are pretty slim, so what's our next step? My challenge is that I have been on a high for almost two weeks straight, and the air is now slowly leaking from my balloon. With my adrenaline rush subsiding, I'm starting to get tired and becoming restless. Pete, on the other hand, is raring to go on, wanting us to come up with a real plan to get back to the East Coast. Pete, I say, I don't want to be running for the rest of my life. He's persistent and wants me to contact my JDL contacts in Los Angeles and get their help, but I don't like the idea. At this point, having always been very emotional, it doesn't take too long before I start to cry. Pete, I've had it, I can't go on anymore. In fact, I don't even know why I ran away in the first place. We go back and forth, finally deciding that it's time for us to part company. Our best option all around is for me to turn myself in to the authorities. Pete, I say, I'll make sure to give you a few hours head start before I turn myself in. This way you can be long gone. We've been together for quite some time, so it's a pretty emotional separation. We've really grown to depend on one another. Hugging each other, we say good-bye and good luck.

As Pete heads for the nearest freeway to make his way back east, I continue to sit in the park. Think Freddy, what do I do now? I need to figure this out. After about an hour of contemplation and bird watching, I decide to head for a nearby movie theater. It's a double feature film, but for the life of me I can't recall what movie I just saw. All I remember is that I've been crying a lot, and not because of the movie. Half the time that I've been sitting here, I've just been crying, the other half regretting that soon I'll have to leave the warmth and comfort of the movie theater. With no other choice, they're kicking me out.

Outside it's gotten really cold, and it's started to rain and get dark. I walk down the street in the same direction I'd come from earlier in the day. Not exactly sure what to do, I see a police car cruising, so I wave them down. I tell them that I'm an escapee from Idaho and wish to turn myself in. To my shock and dismay, they don't believe me, telling me to stop bothering them and go home. I'm really bewildered now and starting to regret parting ways with Pete. Wandering around the streets of San Francisco, I don't know what to do, because even the police don't want me. It's now getting really cold, it's starting to pour, and along with the rain, once again the tears start to flow. I'm all alone and have nowhere to turn.

Needing to get out of the rain, I make a dash for a nearby phone booth. Cold and wet, I sit in the phone booth crying hysterically, feeling so lost. Not knowing what else to do, I decide to call Shelly. Starting with my stint at JINS, we've continued our special sister-brother relationship, and in fact I've received more letters from Shelly than everyone else combined since my incarceration began. Putting in my dime, I call the operator, placing a person-to-person collect call, praying that Shelly will answer the phone and not her mother. Once again, the Lord is with me, and Shelly answers. I'm so lucky because if her mother was home, I'm sure she wouldn't have accepted the charges. As soon as I hear her voice, I break out in tears, telling her what's been going on. Shelly's always been there for me, being one of the very few people in the world I believe truly loves me. She advises me, first and foremost, to find out where the nearest police station is and get there. Tell them you're not leaving until they check out your story, and then just sit there. Half-jokingly, she adds, if that doesn't work, find and pull the nearest fire alarm and then when the fire department responds, you'll for sure get arrested. Wiping away my tears and feeling much better, I say goodbye to Shelly, noticing right nearby a fire department station. Not quite ready to try the false alarm bit, I walk into the fire house and ask where the nearest police station is. Just like my feelings, the rain has cleared a bit, and now I'm determined to make this work. At the Highway Patrol station, I walk straight up to the desk sergeant and explain that I've escaped from a juvenile detention facility in Idaho and I'm turning myself in. Incredible as it sounds, he also doesn't believe me. It's not the first of April, so maybe kids confess to crimes they haven't committed all the time in San Francisco. After a bit of back and forth, the commanding officer finally decides he'd better check out my story. Not knowing if I'm crazy or an ax murderer, they place me in an interrogation room but still don't place me under arrest. Twenty minutes pass as they do their due diligence, until finally two plainclothes cops come in and say, congratulations, you're under arrest. As soon as the cops place me under arrest, my stress level starts to return to normal. One of the greatest fears a human being can face is the fear of the unknown and being arrested is a known for me. I already consider myself a bit of a professional at being arrested, so this whole process of booking and processing is a no-brainer for me.

After the booking process is completed, they tell me I'm to be transferred to the San Francisco County juvenile facility, which is on the other side of the city. After an extremely stressful day, I'm now relaxed. I'm in my comfort zone.

It seems a bit unusual that they haven't yet put me in handcuffs. In fact, other than during the booking procedure they aren't really acting at all, as if I'm even under arrest. The same two cops tell me that they'll be the ones transporting me over to juvenile hall. As we get into their car, they ask me if I'm hungry. Yea, I'm starving. Would you like to go and get a hamburger with us? Feeling a bit more relaxed, I say sure. We pull over at a diner fashioned from an old railroad car and sit in a booth with the jukebox in the background playing, "If You Leave Me Now," by Chicago. This place feels good. It reminds me of the Four Hundred Diner on Broad Street in Elizabeth where Hugh and I used to hang out. When the waitress comes over to take our order, she looks at us strangely. Even though they're in plain clothes, she knows they're cops, but who's the kid with them? The taller one orders for all of us: three burgers, with French fries and Cokes all around.

There's no idle chitchat as we wait for the food to arrive, but the place is far from quiet, between the music from the jukebox and all the comings and goings. I wonder where Pete is now, and if he got away safely. Our food arrives, and it looks and smells delicious; they've even added fried onions. I dig right in, just the way I like it! Mustard, mayonnaise, and Heinz ketchup, the perfect hamburger. I can't believe how friendly the cops out here in California are. I can't imagine the New York cops doing this. I can't believe how hungry I am! Just stuffing my face, I notice that my two new friends aren't eating much. Maybe I'll ask them for their French fries if they're not going to eat them. I start to wonder what's going on. As I'm eating, the chitchat finally starts with them asking me all sorts of innocent questions about all sorts of different things. Taking a bite of my hamburger, I'm answering all their questions eagerly because they're such nice guys. Suddenly, I get a chill up my spine; they're starting to ask questions about my experience with the Jewish Defense League and if I know any of the activists on the West Coast. They mention a couple of people in particular, who in fact I don't know but I've certainly heard their names. Now it's coming together, and although I don't let on, I'm a bit shocked. Not because they're necessarily asking me these questions, but because how do they know about my affiliation with the JDL?

In truth, I really don't know anything or anybody; after all I'm just a kid. That being said, I'm really enjoying my burger and fries, so I start playing them. I must admit that to this day I get a laugh about how gullible these two big city detectives were and how they let a kid play them as I did. After our conversation, which by the way was completely illegal, they drive me over to the juvenile detention center and hand me over to the facility officials.

I'm cool with the whole thing. The incarceration experience here in San Francisco is no big deal for me; I'm an experienced prisoner. I know all about the booking process, and the system in general, and while this is my first foray with the California authorities, it's more or less the same process anyplace you go. Although I'm an escapee in their jurisdiction, which is technically a crime, they certainly don't need the hassle of another juvenile offender. As far as they're concerned, I'm just here to enjoy their hospitality as I await an escort from Idaho to get me back to Edgmead. Put in a private cell, I don't have to deal with the general population, which is fine with me. Knowing more or less what I'm going back to, I can relax and enjoy the solitude. After the past couple of weeks, I can use some rest and relaxation.

In handcuffs, I'm flown back to Boise and immediately transferred back to Edgmead. This time there are no niceties. I'm taken straight to ICU, where I'm put in a special cell reserved for the worst infractions. This of course comes as no surprise to me.

After the initial processing, they start questioning me about everything that took place, from start to finish. Being almost completely honest, I tell them everything, just leaving out the part about the girls and the ranch. For that time period, I had to do some creative storytelling, but I did tell them the whole truth about Pete. At this point it's so irrelevant; he's long gone, and I've no idea where he is now. The funny thing is that Pete was all worried about me giving him enough time to get away, but in the end, the San Francisco authorities never even asked about him.

Because of my previous great record, and also because I'd turned myself in, my sentence in ICU is only five days, but my punishment is far from over. First, obviously I'm now a Form 5, and while there's no negative equivalent of a form 1H, I'm at the bottom of the list for even Form 5s.

Escapes aren't cheap, and I've racked up quite a few expenses during my adventure. The two biggies: retrieval of the car that we stole, and the expenses involved in my return from San Francisco to Idaho. All these costs are far from miniscule, and I have to pay them back by working them off in the kitchen. Every hour not taken up by official nonrecreational activities, I'm expected to work, until I pay off the entire debt. This time I learn my lesson, and I never screw up again, at least not at Edgmead.

Pete is caught six months later and sent directly to juvenile detention in New Jersey to complete his sentence. I never see him again.

**There are times in our lives when things may not be going so well for us, yet we somehow persevere. I wonder how many of those times we had help and didn't realize it. Maybe it's with the help of our hidden angels!**

# Chapter 24

*My idea of Christmas, whether old-fashioned or modern, is very simple: loving others.* **—Bob Hope**

Lots of late hours and lots of hard work, I've finally payed off my escape debt to Edgmead. Keeping my nose clean for the past couple of months, I'm back in everybody's good graces and once again a Form 1H.

Christmas time is in the air, and everybody's feeling the excitement, except for me. Being Jewish, Christmas doesn't have the same meaning for me as for most of the others. Being that this is the first time in my life that I'm not celebrating Chanukah, what makes it even harder is that this year, Chanukah and Christmas coincide. Christmas is always a very slow period with staff taking vacations and many of the residents being granted furloughs to go home. While not the first time that I'm feeling lonely since I arrived, I'm getting pretty depressed. John, my senior unit counselor, sees that something is off with me. Stepping up to the plate, he asks me if I want to spend Christmas day with him and his family.

Although I'm a New York kid who grew up in a traditional Jewish home, I've always enjoyed the Christmas season. I love watching holiday movies and television shows, which always give me warm, fuzzy feelings. Some of my fondest memories are of going with my grandparents to Radio City Music Hall in Manhattan around the holiday season. Besides whatever holiday movie was playing, we'd always see a performance of the world-famous Rockettes, then go out to dinner at a real restaurant. Not having that many wonderful memories from my childhood, seeing everything decorated in the beautiful Christmas decorations always gives me a really warm and fuzzy feeling.

I'm touched by the invitation and tell John that I'd love to come. He not only gets the okay for Christmas Day, but for Christmas Eve as well.

This means I get to stay overnight at his house, which is an amazing treat in itself. What even makes it more amazing is that it's not John's house, but his parents. They live in Coeur d'Alene, a small, beautiful lakeside town in northern Idaho, not far from the Canadian border. John, who I guess is in his early thirties and recently married, will be there with all his brothers and sisters, nieces and nephews. This means that the house will be full to the brim, but their feeling is, the more the merrier.

Always having had a Walt Disney image of what a traditional Christmas is like, Christmas at John's house fits like peanut butter with jelly. It's exactly how I'd always pictured it in my dreams. Tonight's not only Christmas Eve but also the first night I'm sleeping in a real home in a very long time. John's family treat me as one of them. With all the family here for Christmas, I sleep on the couch in the living room, right next to their Norwegian-style stone hearth fireplace, with a nice roaring fire burning. Decorated with the traditional Christmas stockings, the fireplace has one for every member of the household; there's even one with the name "Freddy." John's family is the best, they've thought of everything. With my head full of sugar plum fairies, falling asleep isn't so easy. Completely overwhelmed by their hospitality, I'm just mesmerized by the decorated seven-foot balsam fir Christmas tree. I finally drift off to sleep, listening to the sounds of the crackling log fire in the background. I've never been happier. I don't know if Santa Claus visited that night, but I do know that about six in the morning, I'm awakened by John's seven nieces and nephews, all clambering one on top of the other to get to their Christmas presents.

With one eye open, looking at these little kids so excited and giddy, I feel such a sense of peacefulness and love flow through me as I watch them all opening their presents.

My fairytale story just seems to continue throughout the day. Once the kids are up, it doesn't take long for everybody else to come downstairs and join in the fun. Not only do I receive a Christmas stocking, but Santa Claus also brought me a gift. Receiving a pair of flannel pajamas and matching slippers, I cry as if I'd received a brand-new Chevy Corvette. After the gift opening ceremony, we all sit down to a very hearty, traditional Idaho breakfast consisting of eggs, bacon, sausage, homemade biscuits, and pancakes. It's especially difficult to get up from the breakfast table afterward.

Some of the women stay behind because they want to work on preparing Christmas dinner, but the rest of us head out to Lake Coeur d'Alene to go ice skating. Years ago, my father would take us to Warinanco Park in Elizabeth to ice skate. Because I was always being punished for one thing or another, I didn't get to go that often, but when I did, I really loved it. I've always loved everything about the winter. It's the snow, the cool crisp air, the smells, in fact all the sights and sounds associated with wintertime. After several hours of ice skating, playing in the snow, and just having an unbelievable blast, the children are totally wiped out and ready to go home. The truth is it's not only the kids who are exhausted; we're all pooped. We head back to the house to get some rest and prepare ourselves for dinner.

Christmas dinner at John's house is a formal occasion, a once-a-year event. From A to Z, everything is exactly how I've always imagined a Christmas dinner to be, in fact even better. The table is set with their finest china, everyone is in their Sunday best, and everything is very traditional with all the appropriate trimmings. Not that I'm an expert on traditional Christmas dinners, but it looks like a royal banquet: turkey with stuffing, roast beef, mashed potatoes, gravy, cranberry sauce, and vegetables. Dessert is a feast in itself with an unbelievable variety including pumpkin and apple pie, raisin pudding, and last but not least, traditional Christmas pudding. Every chair has a name card, and I'm seated next to John's younger sister, Sherry, who's five years older than me.

I immediately fell in love with Sherry when I met her last night. She's a dream, and I'm smitten. Five years is a big deal when you're only fifteen, and while she does seem to be fixated on me, it's a totally different fixation than I have for her. Sherry wants to know everything about me, my family, my background, the East Coast, and most of all, what it's like being Jewish. Sherry's a grand talker, and besides lots of questions for me, she's also throwing out some great ideas about all sorts of different things. I don't know why I'm so surprised when seemingly out of the blue she says, Freddy you really don't belong there, you're wasting your time, why don't you go for your GED? In fact, I wouldn't be surprised if you can become a doctor or a lawyer, you're certainly smart enough.

**A general equivalency diploma, better known as GED, is a substitute for a traditional high school diploma. A GED is usually awarded to high school dropouts, who at some point in their adulthood realize that they've made a terrible mistake by not finishing high school. A GED gives them a chance to go back to school for an external course that teaches them the bare requirements, eventually giving them that cherished and often needed high school diploma.**

Sherry, I'm flattered, but with all due respect, you're totally nuts! I barely have an elementary school diploma, and I've never been in high school long enough to drop out. Besides that, I'm only fifteen years old, and locked up in a reform school, to boot!

My Christmas furlough is great although way too short. John and his family were unbelievably kind to me, and Sherry leaves me with quite a bit to think about. I think and think but figure it is a pipe dream. I keep saying no way, but Sherry keeps sending me messages through John, insisting that I speak to the powers at Edgmead. John also won't get off my case, and I finally decide to give it a shot. Usually meant for adults, the official minimum age for the test is sixteen, which is lucky for me because I just celebrated my sixteenth birthday. So, with the insistence and support of John and Sherry, I decide to give it my all. Over the next couple of months, I do whatever is needed to get through the red tape and study. I don't have the knowledge for a lot of it, but the Edgmead teachers help by tutoring me.

Barely sixteen years old and with no real education, I finally take the test, sure that like my school years, I'll fail completely and miserably. To my absolute shock I pass with flying colors.

I'm now a high school graduate.

# Chapter 25

*Of course, we all need angels. I had to have one over my head throughout my life, even right now. The odds of my making it were slim to none. So, you have to have an angel. You have to believe.* **—Michael Oher**

I'm now a real star at Edgmead. The powers have a short memory, conveniently forgetting that John had to fight them tooth and nail to let me take the test in the first place. What does it matter? Not only are they now proud of me, but even better for them, I'm a real success story. Success means they can use my story as a marketing tool. I get it, I'm okay with it, they want to use me to advance their agenda.

But what's in it for me? I've a big ego, very aware that I'm now the flavor of the month, but how can I really use this for my betterment? Now BMOC, I'm a real superstar, but I also know that in the outside world, it doesn't mean a thing. What's so great about someone with a general equivalency high school diploma? It means absolutely nothing! In the short term, I start pushing the envelope as much as possible. Almost anything I can think that is in the realm of possibility, I request. And while my petitions aren't always accepted and they don't always say yes, they seem to say yes more times than no.

All residents at Edgmead, with the exception of those with behavior problems, are entitled to choose an elective. An elective is something unique and personal and may be a hobby or a particular skill one wants to learn. Many of these electives are already taught in house, like for instance, learning how to play a musical instrument, swimming, or even horseback riding. When a resident wants something special, some activity that is not currently in house, he or she has to submit a special petition for approval. Then, like every other petition, the staff weighs the costs versus the benefits of the particular activity, along with the strengths and weaknesses of the applicant. Deciding to really push the envelope, I ask to be allowed to take a course in skeet shooting. In general, and specifically for me, skeet shooting should be out of the question.

Skeet shooting, also known as target shooting, is a sport using shotguns with clay pigeons as the targets. This would be a red flag from any resident, but in my case in particular, with my Jewish Defense League background, it should be a no-brainer. But they approve my petition and I am absolutely shocked once again. I wish I could've been a fly on the wall listening in on that meeting, because I'm sure this one in particular was a blast (pun intended). Bottom line, I learn a new skill and really enjoy learning how to skeet shoot.

I don't remember whose idea it is, or how it comes about, but the powers decide that if I am really going to be a success story, I need to learn social skills. The reasoning is that if I am ever going to make it on the outside, I need to learn how to socialize and get along with "normal" kids. Not as easy as it sounds, considering I'm already sixteen years old and have no formal schooling or classroom skills or etiquette. I do, though, now have a high school diploma.

I don't really have anything to do on campus, other than read. The days are getting warmer and I spend them just roaming around trying to stay out of trouble. I'm not surprised when I'm called in for a special meeting with the director and some of the other senior staff. One doesn't have to be a rocket scientist to know that the Man needs to find something to do with me, especially something that'll tailgate onto my previous success. The main challenge I now have is that I've become overqualified.

Freddy, how would you like to go to a real high school with real kids? Huh? They explain that they've spoken with the Mountain Home High School authorities and arranged for me to attend. Basically, they'd like to use me as a social experiment. The plan is to integrate me into the eleventh grade, hoping that I'll learn the social skills to be able to later blend seamlessly into society. Sounds good to me!

Monday morning arrives, and I'm now an eleventh-grade student at Mountain Home High school. It's a rush being amongst "normal" kids. For the first time ever I'm loving school, especially since I don't have to do any kind of school work because I already have a high school diploma. That being said, in certain respects everything has changed but really nothing has changed. I'm still very different and very out of the box. What's so different here is that I'm "unique," because I come from "that place." In my old life this uniqueness made me the unpopular kid on the block, but here it's just the opposite. It's a feeling I've never experienced before, specifically being liked by the "in crowd." Everyone wants to sit with me at lunch, especially the girls. I wonder if it's because they really like me or because they want to hear all the stories about Edgmead. Or maybe they just think I'm some sort of a side show freak, or perhaps a little bit of all three.

It's a whole new experience for me. I get up every morning with a whole new bounce. Having to start my day off a bit earlier then everyone else, I'm dropped off at school by one of the Edgmead staff and eat breakfast in school. Part of my agreement is that I can't tell any of the kids that I already have a high school diploma. I'm to act as much as possible like every other kid. Having a regular schedule like them, I have a pretty busy day going from class to class. Funny thing, now I enjoy almost every class, and with the exception of trigonometry I'm soaking it in. Besides the regular curriculum, I even manage to get on the wrestling team, which is amazing. I feel a bit like Dr. Jekyll and Mr. Hyde. By day I'm a rather popular high school kid, and at night and weekends, I'm a detainee in a reform school. The real test though is coming up: the junior prom.

My imagination is in overtime mode. Proms and dances have always been a part of my fantasy life, and I'm really excited. I don't have a date, which under normal circumstances would be a disaster, but in my case

I'm okay with it, because just the thought of going is a treat for me. Being that the junior prom is on a weekend night, not part of the school day, I have to submit a petition to the administrative board for approval. I'm not worried. This whole social experiment was their idea, and as expected they give me the okay.

Going to a prom is not as simple as one would think. Not having a date lessens my preparations, but there are still a bunch of things I need to do but don't have a clue as to how. John, who more and more has become my guardian angel, steps in. Junior prom is a black-tie event, which is a new term for me, and I'm really lost, really out of my element. John prepares me, including helping me rent a tuxedo. Explaining all the ins and outs of a prom, he also volunteers to drive me to the school on the night of the prom.

Walking into the school gymnasium, I'm overwhelmed. It's just like in the movies; it's amazing. They've totally transformed the place with colorful balloons and flowers, so you wouldn't even know it was a gym. The lights are dim and there's a really great band playing in the background. I'm nervous and excited and uneasy, and vulnerable. Everybody I see says hello, and some of the kids seem to even go out of their way to greet me. Even though I feel really good, almost as if I truly belong, I still feel like an outsider, like I'm that handicapped kid everybody feels they have to be nice to. I'm that weird kid from that place up on top of the hill known as Edgmead. Along with all my other feelings of inferiority, I'm the only kid here without a date, and the truth be told, I'm really jealous of everyone else.

There's Mary, one of the girls in my class, whom I have a crush on. Mary really likes me, but just as a friend. When I arrive, she gives me that big beautiful smile of hers, mouthing hello to me. Mary is really gorgeous every day, but tonight she's a real knockout. She's dressed in this long elegant light-blue formal gown, topped off with a stunning corsage her date has given her. Looking at Mary, I just want to take her in my arms and give her a big hug. I'm so jealous of her date. So many people around me, but I feel so lonely and out of place. I spend almost the whole first hour at the punch bowl acting like I'm busy doing something. Kids and teachers come over, get a drink and say hello, but I really feel like a bump on a log.

The original euphoria I had when I came is wearing off fast, and I want to go back to Edgmead. I don't belong here; I'm a fish out of water. One of my teachers comes over and asks me if I want to dance with her. Thank you very much, Mrs. Jackson, but no. Persisting, she asks, do you know how to dance? No, not really. Have you ever danced before? Honestly no, I've never even been to a dance before. Taking my hand, she leads me to the dance floor, telling me to relax, that she will teach me. Reluctantly and feeling very queasy, I move to the dance floor with Mrs. Jackson. I feel as if every eye in the gymnasium is upon us.

I stumble at first, but then, closing my eyes, I realize I'm not so bad after all. After a while Mrs. Jackson encourages some of the girls to dance with me, and with each dance I feel more and more at ease. Eventually I even get to dance with Mary, and once again God is looking out for me; it's a slow dance. It's an incredible night.

The more I push the envelope and the more positive experiences I have, the cockier I become. Besides going to Mountain Home High School, a lot of other great things are beginning to happen. One of the things I haven't had to worry about since my incarceration started is money. With all my needs being taken care of, and even getting a small amount of spending money, I haven't thought much about it. In fact, for the first time I'm getting an allowance, but in truth I don't have much opportunity to spend it. That being said, I love money and I love earning it! So I want to get a job. Crazy, another impossibility for a variety of reasons, the most obvious being that I am a convicted juvenile delinquent and still incarcerated. Don't bore me with the facts, what's my next step?

First and foremost, I need to petition the powers, and by this point the staff at Edgmead are used to my outlandish petitions. To their credit they've never laughed at me or said no without due consideration. The truth being that so many of my requests are brand-new ground for them, involving both legal and liability considerations.

As with most of my requests, they don't reject my petition outright. My petition is returned to me with several questions. Where will I be working? What will I be doing? Hours, etc. Their philosophy is that the more information one gives them, the better the chances of getting a yes. When I first arrived at Edgmead, before I had learned the ropes, I would get discouraged with this sort of response, but now the opposite is true. Another valuable lesson I have learnt is that when adults say yes, the answer is yes. When they say no, the answer is no, but when they say maybe, they think they are telling you no, but you hear it as a yes. Finally, if a kid hears it as a yes, then they will turn it into a yes. Using this assumption and logic, and even though I don't have a clear answer, I start looking for a job. In a small town, job hunting for a sixteen-year-old kid isn't easy in general but having to tell them where you live makes it pretty much impossible. Nonetheless I persevere and finally I hit pay dirt. Kentucky Fried Chicken, more commonly known as KFC, needs a part-time dishwasher and is willing to take a chance on me. So back to Edgmead I go with all the details and once again submit the petition. This time, as expected, they give me the go-ahead.

Life is looking up, and I'm really on a roll, almost living like a normal kid. I'm in a real school and have a part-time job, what could be better? One doesn't have to be a rocket scientist to know the advantages of attending high school when you already have a high school diploma, but the disadvantage is that classes are boring and not very memorable. There's one class though that has a lot of importance to me, and that's driver's education. Idaho, being a rural state that relies heavily on farming and ranching, issues restricted driver's licenses at as young as fourteen years old. For daylight hours only, but at sixteen, you can get a regular unrestricted license.

Funny thing is that I didn't have to get permission to take driver's ed, but once I'd passed the class, I had to submit a petition to take the state driving test. Petitioning the committee, I took the driving test and passed. After everything I'd gone through regarding driving and being an unlicensed driver, I'm now officially licensed. Again, a first for Edgmead, and even though they're kind of proud of me, they're smart enough to be a bit leery. And they're right to be. I decide to keep pushing the envelope. Now that I've got a driver's license, a job, and I'm going to school, I petition them to allow me to buy a car. This is a really big one, probably the biggest one yet. Again, they don't outright say no, which is definitely their immediate inclination. Instead they tell me that when I've saved enough money from my job, I should submit a new petition with details.

With all my successes, I'm becoming a real headache to the powers to be. As the saying goes, they're between the proverbial rock and a hard place. On the one hand, how can they possibly allow me to own a car, but on the other hand I'm their major success story. They don't want to stifle my creativity and gusto, but there's no way they can allow me to have a car, so for the time being they decide to play me.

Meanwhile, "back at the ranch," I'm having formal and informal talks about my future. At this point we all know that the status quo won't work for me anymore. According to the original court order that got me sent here in the first place, I'm supposed to be at Edgmead at least for another year. Even if I complete my sentence in full, I'd still only be seventeen, and still a minor. It's pretty much agreed between everyone involved, including me, that the worst thing for me would be to return to my home and/or the East Coast environment. This is even assuming that it's an option, and as far as I'm concerned, it's not. So other than continuing on at Edgmead, what are my options? It's a depressing thought, because as good as the situation is now, I'm still a ward of the State of New Jersey. Under their control and auspices, is that how I'm going to spend the next few years?

Once again, my savior John comes to the rescue when one evening we're talking, and he comes up with this crazy idea: How about going to university? I'm out of the box, always looking for ways to push the envelope, but even I think this is too much! I've come a long way, and I'm street smart, but a general equivalency diploma does not make me educated! Forget it, there's no way! Never say never, says John. Being the great guy, he is, he keeps pushing, getting me to fantasize, and once I do that, watch out! Finally blurting it out, I ask how?

This is too crazy, and this time there are no petitions. John takes the baton by the hand and speaks directly with the powers. Mr. Coons has a connection at Boise State University and arranges for an exploratory interview. This first meeting leads to a number of back and forth meetings involving Edgmead, Boise State University officials, me, and last but not least, the State of New Jersey. No matter what else is decided, at the end of the day, the State of New Jersey is my momma and papa and controls everything, including the purse strings. Finally, all worked out, the university informs me that they'll accept me provisionally for the coming fall semester. The proviso is that I take the ACT entrance exam. ACT is a test for high school students that assesses their mastery of college readiness standards in four separate areas, and Boise State demands a minimum of 75 percent in each area.

I really enjoy fantasizing about going to university, but it's not going to happen. There is no chance I'm going to pass this test, let alone get 75 percent. It's been exciting while it lasted, but there's no way! I've done well, but I've reached as far as I'm going to get in life, and now I've got to deal with it. Perhaps amongst the losers, I'm the best, but the sad truth is that I'm still a loser. I'm pretty much resigned to the fact that I'll remain in a state institution until I'm eighteen.

Although I've given up, thank God once again for the angels like John and a few others who have more faith in me than I do in myself. John convinces Edgmead to get me a tutor to help me prepare for the ACT exams, and for the first time in my life, I'm really studying. I'm still not convinced that I have any chance at all, but what do I have to lose, especially with the fan club I now have. Amazingly, almost everybody at Edgmead, staff and resident alike, are rooting for me to succeed.

The exam, scheduled for the end of June, is nearly a full year since I first arrived at Edgmead, and I'm studying harder than ever before. What am I talking about? I've never studied. I don't even know how to study! How the hell can I expect to pass the test and go to university? This is so futile! I don't believe I really have a chance, but I'm not going to give up. It's not just me, I'm representing all of Edgmead.

My mother always says, busy is good, and boy, am I busy now. Almost every day I'm in school at Mountain Home High, but instead of classes, I'm studying for my upcoming ACT exam. Then most afternoons, I'm at work scrubbing filthy, greasy chicken fryers while at the same time trying to remember dates, facts, and figures that I learnt earlier in the day. Most days I work until closing, taking whatever chicken is left over back to my unit mates. For them, that's the best part of my daily adventure. By this time, other than on the weekends and when I'm sleeping, I'm spending very little time at Edgmead. Of course, I'm still a part of the system, and when I'm there, officially, I'm just like everybody else.

D- day has finally arrived! It's time. The big test is in Boise, and I have to be there bright and early. Because of this, we drove in from Mountain Home last night, staying at the Best Western hotel. This of course is not the first time I've been to Boise, and while it's always a thrill going to the "big city," (population of less than one hundred thousand) this time it's very different.

Day and night, since this whole crazy idea was brought up, I've been fantasizing about going to university and what it'd be like. At the same time, I've convinced myself that there's absolutely no way it's going to happen, but here I am. Today will determine the rest of my life.

I've never seen such a large classroom in all my life. It looks like a small theater, but in fact it's actually a lecture hall. There's almost complete silence as everybody sits at their desks waiting. After checking our ID upon entrance, we're told not to touch the test papers on the desks until so informed. Fidgeting with my No. 2 pencils I've been given, I'm nervous as hell. The exam starts exactly on time, with the proctor giving us the final instructions, saying go! After three hours, I turn in my exam papers, pretty sure I've failed miserably. Even worse, I won't get the results for about a month.

Returning to Edgmead feeling pretty bummed, I hunker down, waiting to see what happens next. With my future in limbo, I first have to wait for the test results, but then what? Regardless of what happens, the powers realize that things can't stay the same and that it's time for me to move on. Shortly after we return from Boise, I'm informed that I'm being moved to the Edgmead halfway house. Not privy to the discussions that led to this, it is my understanding that it is felt that I've outgrown Edgmead. Whether or not I go on to Boise State, I need to be in a different setting.

The halfway house, while still in Mountain Home and still under the Edgmead auspices, is a totally different world. It's more of a short-term facility, mainly used for kids who are close to finishing their sentences. Moving into the halfway house is part of the rehabilitation process, used to ease us kids back into a more normal setting. For the average Edgmead resident, this is usually the first time they start interacting with the outside world. I, on the other hand, am different because even at Edgmead proper, the powers have been looking for all sorts of ways to ease me back into normal society for a while, so for me this is more or less just a geographical move.

In many respects, nothing's really changed, yet I do feel the difference. First of all, I'm in a regular house, in a regular neighborhood, on a regular street. For the first time, I'm sharing a room with just one other kid, and eating my meals in a home dining room, not an institutional dining room.

Everybody here's the same; there are no forms here. None of us wants to break the rules, because if we do, we're simply sent back to Edgmead, or worse. There's zero tolerance here.

While there may be no forms here, the petition system is still very much in place. Having saved enough money to buy a used car, I once again send in my petition. If I was still on the main campus, there'd be no way they'd grant my request, but now that I'm at the halfway house, they're willing to honestly consider it. After much discussion they say yes. Obviously, their agreement comes with a zillion rules and regulations, and I know my car could be confiscated at a moment's notice, with no ifs, ands, or buts, but I'm still willing to take my chances.

My first car is a blue 1964 Ford Falcon station wagon and I'm so proud. I paid three hundred dollars cash for it, and I treat it as my most prized possession, which it is.

With the school year now over, and still waiting on the ACT test results, I tell my new counselor that I want to get a full-time job. Being in the halfway house, there's no need for me to petition for special permission, because it's already part of the program. Edgmead has a work release plan in place, so I get a summer job as a civilian employee working at Mountain Home Air Force base. This is the first time I've ever been on an active military base, and it's like a small town. With almost the exact same population as Mountain Home itself, it's totally self-contained with its own stores, a hospital, a movie theater, a church, and even its own bowling alley. My job is working in a warehouse, packing all sorts of boxes and then shipping them to other air force bases around the world. I've no idea what I'm packing, for all I know they're top-secret weapons, but I could care less. I like the guys here, I'm having lots of fun, and I'm earning decent money. Besides, I've other things on my mind apart from the safety of the free world: What's to become of me?

With a lot more freedom than ever before and no immediate worries, I'm enjoying a sense of stability that I've never known. I'm working, driving my own car, and constantly have money in my pocket, but regardless, I'm still scared. I'm always scared! My fear is, yes, it's all good today, but what about tomorrow? And the next day?

Finished with work for the day, I head back to the halfway house. There's a message for me to not to go to work tomorrow morning but to go straight to the main Edgmead campus for a meeting with Mr. Coons. Yes, the test results are finally here.

The next morning bright and early I'm meeting with Mr. Coons and the rest of the Edgmead administration to receive the bad news. I know I failed, so why am I so nervous? I sit down. Mr. Coons says, we've got good news and bad news. No, they don't ask me which I want first. The good news is that there were four parts to the test: sciences, history, English comprehension, and mathematics. I'd scored well in every area except for mathematics, where I'd failed miserably. I, of course, already know what the bad news is, which is that I'm not going to Boise State. Regardless of how well I did in three of the subjects, I needed a minimum of 75 percent in all the subjects. That being said, I'm absolutely amazed that I did so well in those three subjects. Where did I get the education to actually know the information? But all this is irrelevant now, because it doesn't make a difference. Okay, I understand, so what's in store for me? Can I continue to work at the Air Force Base even after the summer? For the first time since I've known these people, I see them looking at me a bit in shock. They're used to Freddy the fighter, and now I'm totally dejected. Mr. Coons looks at me and says, didn't you hear what I said? You did great in three out of four subjects! Yes, I heard you, but I failed the mathematics part, and the deal was that I had to get a minimum of 75 percent in each subject. With a look in his eyes that I'd never seen before, he looks me straight in the eye and says, Freddy, you fight and petition for everything under the sun. Most of them are crazy and totally out of the box. In the year you've been with us, I've never known you to accept a no, and a number of times you've even gotten yourself into trouble for your stubbornness, and now you're quitting? What happened to you? Why are you willing to give up now? Staring at him blankly while he continues to talk, I'm not fully understanding what he's saying.

I then hear him say, you will not give up! We will not let you! We will submit the test results as is to the university, emphasizing the three parts you excelled in, and ask them to reconsider.

Sounds pretty simple and makes a lot of sense. I should've immediately thought of that, but I guess I'm in shock. Being in shock, you're pretty useless, to yourself and those around you. Thank God again for my angels.

Long story short, we resubmit the request, and after some back and forth, they accept me on a probationary basis. This means I have to maintain a B average for the first year, or I'll be out. I'll worry about tomorrow, tomorrow. Right now, all I care about is that although I'm sixteen years old, uneducated, and a juvenile delinquent, I'm going to Boise State University.

Thank the Lord! Will wonders never cease!

# Chapter 26

*Education is not preparation for life; education is life itself.*
— **John Dewey**


Boise State University, home of the Big Sky Conference Broncos! I need to step back and take a deep breath. How'd this all come about? Where am I?

Today's the first day of the rest of my life, and the butterflies are raging throughout my stomach. Really feeling out of my element, everything is both new and exciting. John's here, helping me find my way around the campus and get acclimated. Assigned to Chaffee Hall, one of the two single male dormitory buildings on campus, I walk into my new room, noticing that my roommate's luggage is already here. Glancing over at the name tags on the bags, I see Jefferey Katz, Concord, New York. Figuring Katz is a Jewish-sounding name, I wonder, did they decide to room the only two Jews on campus together? I know that Jews are sparse on this side of the world, but is this the policy here? Nope, I'm just being a bit paranoid, because it turns out that as far as I can tell, I'm still the only Jew on campus. Jeff shares with me that in Concord there are two different Katz families, the Jewish Katzes and the Catholic Katzes; he's one of the Catholic Katzes. Jeff fits right in: right age, right looks, and an athlete to boot. Also, being Catholic he fits right in with the student population, because the vast majority of the students here are either identifying Catholics or Mormons.

Once again, I'm different. I stand out like a sore thumb, but this time mostly for a good reason. While certainly not a child prodigy, being sixteen years old is still a big deal here. What makes it a little easier is that although I'm only sixteen, I look like I'm nineteen, which is the legal drinking age in Idaho.

Unlike in the penal institutional world where it's hard to keep a secret, nobody here knows my true story. Other than certain top school officials, all everybody else knows is that I'm a sixteen-year-old Jewish kid from the East Coast, which in itself is a rarity here. Everybody is very friendly toward me, especially when they learn I'm only sixteen.

The first few days are taken up by orientation and registration for the classes I'll be taking. Some classes are required courses, others are known as electives, which is more of what specifically interests me. One of my biggest challenges is that I've no choice, I've got to take a math course of some kind, it's a prerequisite. Knowing absolutely nothing about mathematics other than basic arithmetic, I'm stumped. Once again God loves me, and I find a course tailored for the mathematically disabled: Cultural Approach to Math.

Much harder than I'd imagined, university is a real challenge for me. Other than when I studied for the ACT exam, nobody ever taught me how to study, and with no study skills, I'm a real fish out of water. I sign up for the minimum number of required courses, and the rest of my hours are taken up by electives. Slowly acclimating to being on a college campus, I'm really enjoying my new freedom. The only restriction I have at this point is that I have to return to the halfway house on weekends. Although a bit of a pain in the butt, it's really good for my ego having to go back to the halfway house. I feel like a returning hero, and the truth is, I really do enjoy seeing everybody.

The Boise State campus, big, lively, and modern, is like a small town, with pretty much everything I need within walking distance. My dorm room is spacious, with just Jeff and I sharing the room. Every floor has a small kitchenette and lounge, but the kitchenette we only use for snacks or parties, because all our meals are eaten in the cafeteria. The food here is great, and if we're not filled up, there's a great snack bar in the student center. There's lots of other stuff here, everything I need. There's a humungous library, a recreational hall, and amazing sports facilities.

Another big thing here at Boise State is the Greek system, in other words, fraternities and sororities. It all starts with rush week, where one has to be invited by a fraternity member who is referred to as a brother or sister. To even be considered for membership, this member in good standing has to recommend you and agree to become your sponsor. Once an invitation is extended and you're accepted, the rush process begins. During rush week you get to know the brothers in the fraternity house, and basically, it's a time to see if you're a match with them and they with you. The fraternity house, colloquially referred to as the frat house, hosts events like sporting activities, BBQs, and all sorts of parties. Different fraternities and sororities have different reputations and niches that can vary from campus to campus. For instance, the TKEs at Boise State are known to have lots of jocks (athletes), but that's not necessarily true in some of their other campuses around the country. Fraternities and sororities are exclusive clubs. They look for people who have the potential to bond and form friendships, not just while in university, but hopefully for life. Greek life is the terminology for college fraternities' activities, I guess because they're called by Greek letters like TKE, which stands for Tau Kapa Epsilon, or ZBT, Zeta Beta Tau. In the movies, Greek life is portrayed as one big party, but in truth there's much more to it than that. Fraternities and sororities raise several million dollars every year for a host of charities and participate in various philanthropic works. They're also very focused on education and fellowship. In fact, most fraternities and sororities require their members to maintain a minimum grade point average to remain in good standing. That being said, socializing is also a big part of Greek life with parties, formals, and events throughout the year. The chance to meet new friends in an organized atmosphere is a big draw. In addition, older frat brothers will mentor new students who are adjusting to life on campus, and this mentorship is very important. It's certainly very important for me. I don't exactly fit in anywhere, but because I'm so unusual, I'm a draw, and actively being recruited by a number of different fraternities. As with most cultures, the Greek system has its own slang, and instead of being recruited, I'm being rushed, which is the process of recruitment to a fraternity or sorority. Being rushed by a fraternity doesn't necessarily mean I'm a shoo-in, because besides being accepted I have to be vetted. During rush week, we're invited to social events and we're interviewed. Once rush week is over, the fraternity brothers vote on to whom they want to extend an invitation. Once an invitation is extended and accepted, you're considered to have "pledged" the fraternity or sorority, thus beginning the pledge period. For me it comes down to either the TKEs or Sigma Phi Epsilon, known as the Sig Eps. While the TKEs seem to be a great bunch of guys, they're mostly jocks. The Sig Eps also have their share of jocks, although not as many, but more important, I feel an instant chemistry and accept the invitation.

Becoming a pledge doesn't necessarily mean that I'll ultimately be accepted as a full-fledged member. Pledge period lasts a couple of months, and during this time we participate in almost all fraternity activities, other than voting or holding office. The pledge period is about answering two simple questions: Am I for them, and are they for me? This is taken very seriously, because if all goes well, I'll be sworn in as a brother, and a brother is for life.

Greek life isn't for everybody, but I take to it like a fish to water. Almost from the start I bond with these guys, some of whom grow into lifelong friendships. Sigma Phi Epsilon is the second oldest fraternity in the country and has chapters all over the world. This makes me feel that I'm part of something bigger than just me. As universities vary from location to location, so do fraternities. While there are certain chapters in the United States that are predominantly Jewish, here again I'm the lone Jew, and in fact, similar to the demographics of the university, most of the brothers are either Catholic or Mormon. I really love these guys and feel more at home than perhaps at any other time in my life. As great as I feel, though, I'm constantly worried, because I know that I'll be vetted, that it will all fall apart, and I won't be accepted.

Going through pledge period is lots of fun but also a major pain in the rear. Good or bad, the main thing about me being part of the Sig Eps is that I instantly have a home and a social life. Unlike the movies, hazing here is neither dangerous nor completely humiliating. It's good clean fun, although sometimes it can, to say the least, be a bit uncomfortable. There are certain traditional methods of making sure one is worthy of becoming a fraternity brother, and while some of it may seem foolish to outsiders, I have no regrets. Becoming a Sig Ep is one of the best decisions I've ever made.

It's exhausting, and between school and fraternity activities, it's never hard for me to fall asleep. Another long day, I quickly fall asleep, when seemingly out of nowhere, I'm awakened by being dragged from my bed. Just wearing underwear, I'm thrown into the back of a blacked-out van. This has gotta be some sort of a crazy nightmare, like I'm being kidnapped by the CIA. I've had nightmares like this before, where I'm sure it's real, but sooner or later I wake up. Yelling for help, I'm searching for a way out, but it can't be a dream because I now hear others screaming. Slowly, as the cold air starts to ease through my brain, I realize that I am in fact being kidnapped, but not by the CIA. I get it! I can now recognize the other yelling voices, and it hits me. It's the three of us pledges, and we must be undergoing some sort of hazing ritual.

Waking up to some sort of understanding of what's going on, I realize that the reason I'm freezing is that I'm wearing nothing but my underwear. Calming down and realizing that my life isn't in danger, I accept the inevitable. After being driven about twenty miles out of town, the van stops on a lonely country road. Our masked captors let us out of the van, giving each of us a bag with a bottle of Coors beer, a bag of pretzels, and our shoes. Without saying a word, they drive off. We understand our mission is to get back to the fraternity house as quickly and painlessly as possible. Definitely wasn't easy, and definitely very embarrassing, but eventually, working together, the three of us make it back.

Besides the internal pranking, which is part of Greek life, there's also quite a bit of rivalry and competition with the other fraternities. These are not just about pranking each other, but also about trying to best the other fraternities in sports contests and philanthropy drives. We do many things to raise money for charity, and we're always striving to be the best in everything we do. I love being part of Greek life in general and the Sig Eps in particular. Here, I'm part of something important.

Right before the Thanksgiving holiday, three events happen that have a major effect on my future. First off, I'm reminded that while I may have some really good friends, I'm still alone, without family. My grandmother passes away, and I'm the only one of my siblings not at the funeral. Second, upon the advice of Sherry, I petition the Edgmead review board, asking that the restriction of having to return on weekends be lifted. It's granted. Lastly, using the traditional blackball voting method, I'm voted in as a new fraternity brother.

Now I'll be going through a very old, traditional, and secret ritual of initiation to become a full-fledged Sigma Phi Epsilon fraternity member. In my past, membership in a tightly knit group usually meant you were either part of a gang or, in my case, the JDL. In retrospect, while I'm very proud of my involvement with the Jewish Defense League, I don't think it was necessarily the healthiest thing for a child, but this is healthy. Not only am I having a great social life, but I've healthy mentors. Some of my mentors are older students, like JD who's a senior and star quarterback for the Broncos. JD is truly someone to look up to. Although courted by the National Football League to play professional football, he gave it up to go on to medical school and become a doctor. Or perhaps Micky, the sports trainer for the football team who as a Sig Ep alumnus is our faculty advisor.

**I'd meet many fraternity members over the years, who from the moment they found out that I was a fellow Sig Ep member would immediately treat me as a brother. One of my favorite memories is attending one of the annual Sig Ep alumni conferences. Sitting around smoking cigars and drinking whiskey, a few of us are playing a friendly game of poker. Who joins us but the world-famous actor**

**Carrol O'Conner, who happens to also be a Sig Ep alumnus, from the University of Montana.**

While fraternities by their very nature are all about brotherhood, women are an integral part of Greek life, and that's where sororities come in. While there's no formal arrangement, many times a certain fraternity and sorority will naturally just form a unique bond and partner up both officially and unofficially. Such is the case between the Sig Eps and Delta Delta Delta, also known as the Tri Deltas. While I have many good female friends, some of my best are with the girls from Tri Delta, many of them becoming really close. Unfortunately, "friends" is the key word! Because of my age, the girls feel that I'm no threat and are comfortable confiding in me their deepest darkest secrets. The challenge with most platonic relationships is that at least one of the couples tends to want a bit more, and unfortunately, I'm usually that person. On the one hand, it really does boost my ego to have so many beautiful and older women want to be friends with me, even sometimes best friends. My challenge is that even though they're all crazy about me, sometimes my feelings turns into a crush, which complicates our friendships.

Much of the social life in universities revolves around booze, whether it's at a party, a bar, or even a pizza parlor. The drinking age in Idaho is nineteen, but I rarely have a problem getting into bars because I look much older. So many of the times that we go to bars, my friends who are of drinking age are the ones who get carded, and me they just wave by.

Quickly evolving from a juvenile delinquent into a normal college freshman, it's hard to tell me apart from the other students. Everything's going great, but fear is still raising its ugly head and I can't stop worrying that somehow my secret will be discovered.

# Chapter 27

***I never knew what I was missing, until I experienced it. —
Roochie Fishel Sinai***

Money is not an issue for me, because all my expenses are covered by
the New Jersey State taxpayer, but it's a double-edged sword. For all
intents and purposes, I'm on a long leash that the authorities hold. I
constantly have to report back to them and am in constant fear that they'll
jerk my chain at any time. Sometimes I get complacent, thinking I'm
completely free, but then something happens to pull me back to reality.

Early spring, the Edgmead authorities, in conjunction with one of the
local television affiliates, think it'd be a great idea to do a documentary
television program on Edgmead. The program is supposed to be about
Edgmead in general, and my story in particular. I'm not really happy
about this, because none of my friends are aware that my umbilical cord
is attached to Edgmead and the New Jersey state authorities. This means
telling my story to the world, and of course all my new friends. Do I want
them to know exactly who I am and where I come from? They tell me
that this documentary is important and is meant to show the world that
the extra money spent on places like Edgmead is a worthwhile
investment for the taxpayer. Look at your story, they say, you've
progressed from being a juvenile delinquent living out of a stolen car to
a successful college student. I'm torn as what to do. I can always say no.
Nobody can force me to do this. At the end of the day, they still need my
permission, but I'm afraid that if I refuse, it may come back to haunt me
later. On the other hand, who doesn't want to be a star? In 1977 there are
only three or four television channels in Boise, and if someone is on
television, everybody knows about it. I know that once my story is out
there for the whole world to see, it will not only be embarrassing for me
but might open me up to ridicule. With very mixed feelings, I acquiesce.

Wow, do I get a shock! The truth is that at the end of the day, it ends up improving my stature everywhere I go. I become an instant hero on campus. Sure, I am different and that hasn't changed, but now my friends look at me in a totally new light. It feels good, not just with my friends but in general. I come across people who recognize me from the broadcast, who compliment me on my success. Once again, I'm a BMOC.

My social life improves immensely, but still not my love life, which is virtually nonexistent. Blessed with loads of friends, I still can't get rid of this feeling of loneliness. It seems that all my buddies are involved with someone or have an active dating life. I'm dying to date someone, anyone, but all the girls I know just want to be good friends, some even considering me their best friend. Eddie is my best guy friend, and Julie, my best girl friend. Both of them are nineteen and although there's no connection between them, I'm in love with them both. Eddie's a fantastic guy, my fraternity brother. His passion is cooking and he's working his way through school as a sous chef in one of the finest hotels in Boise. Julie is studying nursing, and I have the biggest crush on her, but she only sees me as a great friend. She really loves me; in fact she describes me to her friends as her younger brother. Unfortunately, this now is the story of my life.

Not lacking in experience with the opposite sex, true romance still eludes me. Probably some of my experiences should have come a little later in life, when I was a bit more mature, but I've still never had a real romantic relationship, and I'm lonely. What makes it worse is that everybody around me seems to have someone, and many of my girlfriends, especially Julie, are involved in relationships. It's so frustrating, she confides in me her deepest and darkest secrets, while not realizing that I've a heavy crush on her. Patrick, one of my fraternity brothers is planning on going into the priesthood. Maybe I should join him. I'm definitely getting the right experience: no female companionship and listening to confession.

One evening we're drinking beer at the Ram's Head, a major hangout for the university crowd, when this young, attractive woman starts chatting me up. I'm really excited. That is, until one of my buddies, trying to brag on me, tells her how old I am. In a flash, she's out of there. Bummed, I notice Julie hanging out at another table with her boyfriend, and I just want to cry.

Not having girls my own age around, this type of frustration continues to haunt me. While once in a while I do get a date, I can't seem to really connect to girls in the way I want to.

Other than the "girl situation," my freshman year is great, and even though I don't need to work, my entrepreneurial drive takes over. Still being on a leash, I have to get permission from the Man for anything considered out of the ordinary, and getting a job falls into the "out of the ordinary." The main concern of the powers is whether it will affect my studies. When I assure them that it'll have absolutely no negative effect, they give me permission with the proviso that if my grades suffer, I'll have to quit. My grades don't suffer because they're lousy to begin with. Nobody understands that regardless of how bright I am; I've never been taught study skills.

Whether it's studying, taking exams, or even having the patience to sit in class, these are skills I've never learnt. The skills I've learned over the years are survival and communication, and that's what's gotten me this far. My survival skills have taught me to do whatever it takes just to get by.

With the okay from Edgmead, it's time to find a job and start building wealth. My dream is to be a millionaire by the time I'm twenty-one, which means I've got four years. That being the case, I need to get my butt in gear. As I'm now seventeen, and a student at Boise State, it's much easier to find work than when I was a resident of Edgmead. Walking into an office supply warehouse, I easily get hired part-time as a stock boy. It's as boring as a job could be, and I quit after a couple of months, quickly finding another job. Now working for a collection agency, I hound people into paying their bills. Not boring, but I really hate this job, so I quit after just two weeks, never even going back for my paycheck. With no lack of employment opportunities but a bit discouraged, I move on to my next job as a bus boy at the Black Angus Steak House. Bingo, this job I really love! Soon, even though it's unusual because I'm not yet eighteen, they advance me to a waitering position. This is a really big deal! I love serving people, and the customers love me. How do I know they love me? Tips, lots and lots of tips.

My life has turned into a fairytale. Never even imagining that life could be this good, every day seems to lead to something else new and exciting. Fairytale, yes, but I still can't shake the boogieman; I'm still always scared that any day the roof will crash in on me and I'll find myself all alone again. Embarrassed and ashamed about some of the things I've done in the past, I'm constantly in a state of fear that my friends will find out the truth about me. Yes, they now know about Edgmead and my JDL activities, but there's so much more that I'm ashamed of, stealing the car, for instance.

Sometimes it feels the burden is too much for me. Even with great friends I've nobody to really confide in. It's crazy, my life has never been better, but I'm now getting a bit suicidal. I don't mean really suicidal, or maybe I do? I just feel that it'll all come crashing down and then what? A year away from eighteen and adulthood, but who will take care of me then? What will I do? Where will I go? Can I handle the humiliation?

Not knowing what to do, and looking for some release, I start gambling. I love the action, wagering on almost everything I can. Winning sometimes, but losing most of the time, I don't care, because it's the action I crave. As long as I'm busy, I don't have time to think, and thinking for me is bad. In fact, I've got the thinking disease. I absolutely think too much. When I think, I get depressed, and that's dangerous, so I've consistently got to find new and exciting things to keep me busy all the time.

Besides my thinking disease, I've another challenge. Having learnt the art of survival from a young age, I've become something of an expert. Being constantly in survival mode means never being able to completely relax. Survival mode means always having my antenna attuned to trouble, and because of this I'm constantly on an adrenaline high. Sometimes this translates in a positive way, and sometimes negative, but my real challenge is that I need action all the time. I just can't relax and chill out.

One of the few evenings I finish work early, I go by the fraternity house and see Eddie and Tim hanging out on the front porch, drinking beer. In jest I say, I'm bored, let's drive to Reno and play some blackjack. Reno, Nevada, known as "The Biggest Little City in the World," while not Las Vegas, is a big gambling town. Much closer to Boise than Las Vegas, it's still not exactly a place you just go on a whim. Eddie and Tim, sure that I'm joking, say, sure let's go to Reno. Playing the classic dare game, waiting to see who folds first, we get into my car. Driving on I-80, we're all just waiting for the other to say, enough! None of us really believes we're going to Reno, after all it's a minimum six-hour drive. We can't be going because we all have school the next day, and I also have work. Nonetheless, I'm still driving. After about an hour, Eddie is starting to get a little worried. We're not going to Reno, we can't be going to Reno. Laughing, I know we're just playing him, because I know there's no way we're really going to Reno, but I keep on driving. Nobody has the guts to pull the plug, and before we know it, it's three in the morning and I see blue lights flashing in my rearview mirror. Pulled over by the police for speeding. Eddie, finally realizing we weren't going to stop, had fallen asleep in the back seat. Startled when the cop shines his powerful flashlight into the backseat, Eddie wakes up and asks, where are we? It's a Nevada state trooper who responds, saying that we're about forty-five minutes outside of Reno. At this point there's no doubt in any of our minds that we're going to Reno. One hour later, after receiving my speeding ticket for going thirty miles over the speed limit, we're at the craps tables in **the Sundowner Hotel and Casino**. Having hardly had any sleep, we have a great time! We drink a little, gamble a little, and sleep a little before heading back to Boise.

Addicted to action, I miss a big exam and fail. Of course, I also miss work that night, even knowing that my irresponsible behavior will bring repercussions. I just can't seem to help myself. It's as if I've got some secret desire to fail. It's not that I don't care, I really do, but it still doesn't stop me from sometimes doing stupid things. In spite of my stupidity, I'm lucky because I call in sick at the last minute, and they don't fire me.

**There's not one day of my life in which I believe I've failed, but many a day, I've just quit.**

# Chapter 28

***Summer love is the stuff Hollywood dreams are made of.***
**—Anonymous**

With the spring semester about to end, I need to think about summer plans. As far as living arrangements, I've two options. First option, home to New Jersey, which as far as I'm concerned isn't going to happen. It's not that I don't want to go home, in fact I really miss my siblings and would love to see them, but I know I'm not wanted. For my younger siblings, whom I haven't seen in over two years, I'm more of a myth than anything else. I did see Bethy and Dinny last summer, when Mommy took them on a cross-country vacation, and they stopped in Idaho to visit me. We exchange letters from time to time. They're all very proud of me, but for the life of me, I can't understand why. Perhaps they've never been told the extent of my escapades, but regardless, they're always bragging about their older brother to their friends. It's got to be challenging for them, because the stories they tell are so farfetched that their friends have trouble believing that there even is an older brother.

If going home is not a realistic option, the only alternative is the halfway house in Mountain Home. It's not such a bad option. It feels like home, and besides, I have my car. In fact, I just bought a new car, a small sporty Mercury Bobcat with a hatchback, only three years old.

Returning to Edgmead and the halfway house, I feel like a conquering hero. In many ways I feel more at home at Edgmead than anywhere else. Thanks to Edgmead, I've a job for the summer at a local mobile home factory. Pretty boring job, but the money is fantastic, and the hours are great. Working on an assembly line from seven in the morning until three in the afternoon, we build four mobile homes every day. If we manage a fifth, we get a big bonus. Finishing work at three and only having to be back at the halfway house at eleven p.m., I've got all day to hang out.

Summer time in Idaho is beautiful, the weather is great, and I find myself more at peace than I've been all year. Here I don't have to put on airs; it's easier to be myself in this environment. Mr. Coons has a couple of trips planned for the summer for the 1H group, and I'm invited to both of them.

Grand Teton National Park is in the northwest part of Wyoming and encompasses the Teton mountain range, the 4,000-meter Grand Teton peak, and the valley known as Jackson Hole. We've set up camp on the western shore of Jackson Lake, which is an undeveloped part of the lake, having only hiking trails and a handful of primitive camping spots. The stunning picturesque lake surrounded by beautiful mountains and lush forests is one of the largest high-altitude lakes in the United States. The lake is loaded with a number of different types of fish species, including all sorts of lake trout and mountain whitefish, and we fish every day. The best part is, what we catch, we eat.

After sleeping under the stars, we wake up to the smell of bacon, eggs, and freshly caught trout. Besides fishing, we do lots of boating, swimming, and hiking. In fact, there are over fifteen islands in the lake including the largest, Elk Island, where we have a blast.

Probably the best summer in my life, the cherry on top is Vicky. Vicky, my first mature love, is also seventeen, from New Jersey, and from a socioeconomically upper-class family similar to mine. She arrived at Edgmead about a year ago, right before I left to go to the halfway house, so I didn't have a chance to meet her until now. She's about to complete her sentence and is now also in the halfway house, being transitioned to go home in September. We hit it off from the start, enjoying each other's company and having lots of fun together. Vicky is smart, funny, and beautiful, and I'm in love. Suddenly life takes on a whole new meaning for me. We're together all the time and we can't keep our hands off each other. One of my coworkers at the mobile home factory, who's old enough to be my father, is always giving me his negative views on life.

A jaded fellow, he tells me not to get too excited, that it's only mere infatuation. He may be right, but when I look into her eyes my heart flutters and I feel nervous and excited at the same time. They say that all good things must come to an end, and we part company at the end of the summer. Vicky and I promise to stay in touch, but we don't, and I never see or hear from her again.

# Chapter 29

*Be careful what you wish for.* —Anonymous

Back at Boise State for my second year, I've the option of living in the fraternity house. While still at the halfway house during summer vacation, I petitioned the administrative board at Edgmead for permission to move from the dormitory, and they agreed. *Animal House*, a hysterically funny film about living in a fraternity house, was released about a month ago, and is already a smash hit. While the Sig Ep house isn't exactly Animal House, there are definitely similarities, and for me, it's an exciting place to live.

Even though the summer's changed me in some ways, here at Boise everything's pretty much the same. Socially great, academically just barely getting by. When asked what I want to do after my studies, I audaciously say that my plan is to eventually go to law school. It's really just a fantasy, as I'm hanging on by a thread. Even though I'm majoring in political science, I don't have to declare a specific field of study until my third year. For the time being, I'm taking the basic required courses to get by, but I'm also taking lots of electives that interest me, like skeet shooting, bowling, and swimming.

Everyday life—mundane, routine, natural, habitual, or normal—is definitely not me. Once again having the itch, I start looking for a job. Barb, one of my friends from the Tri Delta sorority, is the manager of the local drive-in movie theater and offers me a job as assistant manager. Great title, but in truth this means I do a little of everything, most of the time working in the box office or the snack bar. I have loads of fun, make new friends, and get to watch all the movies for free.

As usual, I'm in love, and once again it's one sided. Working with Barb every evening, I've got a huge crush on her. Barb, being three years older, has no interest in me other than being just friends, and besides, she's got a boyfriend. I'm so jealous of Charles, not only because he's dating Barb, but he's also an investigator for the Idaho Bureau of Investigation. Most painful for me is that Charles is a great guy, having everything I ever dreamt of. Barb and Charles, like so many of my friends, some of whom will be graduating at the end of the year, are planning on getting married after graduation.

Living in the frat house and working at the drive-in, the fall semester is moving on, and once again, my life is quite busy and exciting. With memories of Vicky fresh in my mind, I constantly pine for a girlfriend, and this stresses me out. Even though I'm real busy, I'm once again feeling agitated, and that familiar need for an adrenaline rush again starts flowing throughout my body.

**I've learnt throughout my life that when one wants something bad enough, the stars will align, giving you exactly what you're looking for. That's exactly what happened to me but be careful what you wish for.**

One afternoon, as the stars are busy aligning, I'm walking through the student union building on the way to the library. My curiosity is piqued by a recruitment table set up by the United States Army. Venturing over, I find out that the military has a shortage of nurses and engineers and are recruiting for such. No, they say, you don't have to be presently involved in either area of study, but of course, if interested, I'd need to be willing to change my course of study. Interesting as it all sounds, I'd also have to pass the necessary exams and criteria, which seems like so much of a complication, I'm getting a headache just thinking about it. Continuing on to the library, I don't give it another thought.

Thursday evening the movie *Grease* is top billing, and I'm working in the snack bar when two soldiers order popcorn and drinks for four. Curious, I start chatting with one and picking his brain. Certain that I couldn't pass muster anyway, I try to put the idea out of my mind. I can't, and the idea starts my juices flowing. Unable to get the idea out of my head, I start to visit the recruiting offices of the various branches of the military. Each branch tries to outdo the other with their different programs, but only the army has this specific program that would allow me to have my cake and eat it too. The coast guard and navy are definitely out of the question, the marines are too tough for me, and while the air force is a possibility, it still doesn't sound as good as what the army's offering. The army's program is very similar to the Reserve Officers Training Corps (ROTC), specifically for registered nurses and civil engineers. The program is that if one agrees to take one of these courses of study, the US Army will pay all expenses for your entire education plus a small monthly stipend. For this generous offer, one would have to make a commitment of several years of active and reserve military service.

Along with any academic challenges I might have, I of course have another small problem. Though I've made it this far, I'm still a minor, and the State of New Jersey is still my momma and papa. Being almost eighteen years old would normally mean that I'm about to legally become an adult, but in my case that's not necessarily true. Technically, the state can decide otherwise, holding on to me until I'm twenty-one, and it's still not sure what they intend to do. Up to now I haven't really worried about it, because even if they keep me under their jurisdiction, the upside is that they'll have to continue paying my tuition and living expenses. Now, though, if I get them to release me, I'll have my cake and eat it too, because I'll get the Army to cover most of my expenses. A lot to think about, but at this point it seems academic since I'm getting lousy grades and the army's academic criteria is a B average, minimum. Except for the one time Mr. Coons got on my case, I've always been proud of not taking no for an answer. Priding myself as being a go-getter, I know that if I truly want something, I'll get it. So, I make a decision. I simply refuse to give up. I'm going to make this work! I'm going to join the United States Army as a registered nurse-in-training. Nursing? I'm going to become a lawyer, or at the very least some kind of businessman, but a nurse? Yeah, but they don't want lawyers or businessmen in the army, at least not right now. So, having the army bug, it's gotta be nursing or engineering, and engineering is definitely out of the question. First, I've absolutely no interest in engineering, and second, I'd need to take lots of mathematics courses, which, to put it mildly, is not my strongest point. Nursing on the other hand, although not necessarily a career I'm interested in, is a field of study I think I can find exciting. Also, with a nursing degree, I rationalize to myself, I could still go on to law school. Lastly, my father, while not himself a Holocaust survivor but a product of that generation, would always drive home to us kids that a Jew should always have skills that could be used on the run, and nursing certainly falls under that category.

Now that I've made the decision, I have to figure out how to overcome the roadblocks, the first of which are the state authorities. It's been a long time since we last spoke, but I decide to call my mother to brainstorm with her. Whatever differences I have with Mommy, she's a genius, and I know she wants the best for me. She thinks it's a great idea, and she's sure Abba will love the idea as well, so she agrees to take it up with my state caseworker and see what can be worked out.

At the end of the day, with my parents' blessing, the state not only agrees to release me from being under their tutelage, but they also encourage the army officials to look the other way about my grade point average. Looking the other way would be illegal, so it's not something they can do, but there's another not widely heard of program that can make this whole thing work. This is assuming, of course, I can pass the rest of the entrance requirements. The deal proposed is that I take my military training in scheduled increments, while doing my academic work both at Boise State and the Academy of Health Sciences, a military college located in San Antonio, Texas. My commitment would be various stints of active duty and then six years of active reserve.

Everything is more or less worked out, but because I'm still not yet eighteen, I have to physically go back to New Jersey to officially be released by the state, as well as complete the paperwork for my induction into the army.

A bit more than three years after I ran away, I'm going home to Elizabeth for Christmas break. To say that this is all very strange for me is an understatement. Never thinking I'd see Elizabeth again in general, and Denman Place in particular, I'm asking myself, is this even my home anymore?

Flying back into Newark airport is very different; this time I'm flying unescorted. My caseworker is there to greet me and take me home. It doesn't feel as if it's my home, and as far as I'm concerned, I'm just a visitor passing through my parents' house. I'm scheduled to be here for about fourteen days. Nobody really knows how this is all going to fall out, but here I am. When I walk into the house, my mother gives me a perfunctory hug and my father actually shakes my hand. My siblings look at me as if I'm a stranger. Bethy and Dinny are both going to schools away from home, coming home on weekends, and my three younger siblings, Rachel, Zev, and Chana Szenesh, are living at home. They look great, and it's so good to see them. The first few days back are very strange, the tension very heavy, but life seems to move on. I go for some really long walks, rediscovering my old hunting grounds, but I don't miss Elizabeth at all. The truth is I feel so out of place here; it's not my home anymore. Bonding with my younger siblings is really special, but knowing my stay here is to be very short, I can't help but tear up every time I think about how much I've missed them. Wondering when I'll see them again, I'm also spending lots of time talking to Mommy, which is a new experience. I can't remember the last time we really talked, if ever, and meanwhile Abba more or less ignores me, which is fine with me. Chanukah and Christmas coincide this year exactly, so I'm spending all the December holidays at what was once my home. Splitting my time between friends and family, I find this whole experience very strange. It seems like a lifetime ago when I last saw these people, and while everybody's really nice to me, I know that I no longer belong. Besides friends and family, I need to focus on the real reason I'm in New Jersey, which is sorting out my business with both the state and federal authorities. I'm not counting my chickens yet. Even though everything has supposedly been sorted out, until it happens, it hasn't happened, and nothing can happen until the fourth of January when I officially turn eighteen.

Who would've believed it? January 4, 1979, a Thursday, and I'm finally eighteen years old and legally an adult. The next day, I'm officially released from the custody of the State of New Jersey. Monday morning, January 8, I sign my enlistment papers, and the following day I'm on the plane headed back to Boise, but now I'm legally an adult, and a free man!

# Chapter 30

*Great things never came from comfort zones. —*
**Anonymous**

A party of a lifetime: kegs of beer flowing, all sorts of delicious munchies, my fraternity brothers really know how to throw a party, and what a party it is. Perhaps I'm exaggerating a bit, but it seems like half the university has dropped by the fraternity house to wish me good luck on my upcoming military journey.

Up for almost forty-eight hours partying, and although I'm wiped out, I'm sure this will be one of the greatest memories I'll ever have. Ordered to report Monday morning to the Military Entrance Processing Center in Boise, I need to be there at 0700 hours, and my fraternity brothers have insisted on taking me. Monday, March 10, 1980, not quite five in the morning, still pitch-black outside, and freezing with snow still on the ground, it's time to head out. But the front steps of the Sig Ep house are blocked and impossible to pass. It seems that sometime during the night, someone plastered a humongous poster signed by all the girls from Tri Delta wishing me good luck and bon voyage. I'm so freaking blessed. I've such great friends.

My brothers think of everything, and because there are forty of us, they've rented a bus for the occasion. Our first stop is Denny's restaurant for breakfast, and after being served forty portions of their triple grand slam breakfast, we drive toward the induction center on Bannock street. The staff sergeant at the front desk is in shock. He doesn't understand what's going on and calls for assistance. They've never seen such a huge sendoff, and they're impressed! It's an awesome sendoff, with each one of my buddies wanting to hug me, but finally the sergeant kicks them all out and directs me to where I need to go. Taken to a room for my final physical examination, I start to learn the famous military saying, "hurry up and wait." Once I get the medical okay, I'm sworn in as a member of the United States Armed Forces. It's now official; I'm a soldier in the United States Army.

The biggest challenge with waiting is that it gives me too much time to think, and in this case, thinking is bad! What have I done? Am I out of my mind? What's a nice Jewish boy like me doing in the army? Can I handle it? Will it be too tough, and will they throw me out? Perhaps I'll really screw up and end up in the stockade.

The day is broken up with all sorts of induction activities, but most of my time is spent just waiting, thinking, and sweating. There are probably close to a hundred guys here, not all from Boise, and not all going to the army. The United States Armed forces are made up of five different branches; army, navy, air force, marines, and coast guard, and we're all heading to different branches of service. Except for a few remarks here and there, and some crude jokes, we're pretty much ignoring each other. Whether we admit it or not, we're all thinking and worrying about the same things. About noon, they hand out sack lunches, but we've no time to eat because the buses are waiting outside to take us to the airport. Although most of us are not going to the same place, we're all starting our journey from the Boise airport. At the airport, we quickly separate as we're sent to different gates, depending on our final destination. My orders have been cut for Fort Leonard Wood, Missouri, where I will do my basic training.

Upon arrival in Saint Louis, I settle down in the USO lounge for a long wait. The Saint Louis airport is three hours away from Fort Leonard Wood, and I need to wait until all the other recruits from all over the United States arrive.

Finally, at about eight in the evening, we're loaded on to buses for our trip to our final destination. I figure we will arrive at about eleven p.m., so I try and get some sleep, but even though I'm totally exhausted, I can't fall asleep, and the closer we get to Fort Leonard Wood, the more stressed out I'm getting.

Looking around at the different guys on the bus, I think about how they're all from different places all over the United States, but yet headed toward the same destination. The same destination, yet all so different. Different races, shapes, and sizes, and of course religions. I guess the two things we all have in common is that we are all United States citizens, and we're all probably nervous about what lies ahead of us.

As the bus comes to a screeching halt at Fort Leonard Wood, almost instantaneously the front door opens, and we're being yelled at. I don't know who's in charge or what I'm supposed to be doing, but whoever "they" are, they're starting to instill the fear of God in me. Getting off the bus, the very first words I hear is hands out of pockets! and I learn very quickly that real men don't put their hands in their pants pockets. The purpose of your pants pocket is to either put something in or take something out. That's rule number one. Rule number two is that a recruit never just walks anywhere, he either better be running or better look like he is. Rule number three is that we're no longer recruits, we're trainees, and trainees are the lowest form of life on the evolutionary scale. Finally, rule number four, which is the most important rule, is never to question the army or your higherups; they're always right and a trainee is always wrong.

As rough as it is being a trainee, I guess it's a lot better than being a detainee. In reality, rather than the State of New Jersey being my momma and papa, now it's the United States government. Just like before, I don't have to worry about any of my materialistic needs, and I mean nothing. Everything I need is taken care of by my new momma and papa. Even though it's after eleven and we're totally exhausted, the army is not going to let us go to bed on an empty stomach. Marched to the mess hall for a late-night supper, I'm much too nervous to eat, but I've got to admit, the food looks really good. After a quick supper, in complete silence we're marched to the temporary barracks that will be our home for the next few days. It's the wee hours of the morning, very dark, and I'm totally exhausted, but I still manage to get the feel and look of our barracks. Just like in the movies, the barracks are old World War II–style. Everything in the army is either fast or "hurry up and wait," usually a combination of the two. We're quickly assigned to our bunks and told to hit the sacks, because morning comes real early in the army. Like every other place I've ever been, here once again I need to learn a whole new language and culture.

Wakeup call in the army is called reveille, and indeed comes real early; 04:30, to be exact. Even though we're all still exhausted, nobody dares sleep in, and just in case we don't hear the bugler, a bunch of drill sergeants' barge into the barracks, screaming at us to get up and out. Ordered to be dressed and outside in formation in fifteen minutes, I feel like I've just put my head down on the pillow. As I'm having a little trouble getting out of bed, one of the drill sergeants decides to assist me. He simply flips the mattress over, with me still on it, and wonder of wonders, I get up. Fifteen minutes later, after a stampede to the bathroom, I'm standing in the freezing cold with about one hundred other guys in some sort of formation. The truth is that most of these guys probably never even heard of the word formation.

Early March in Missouri can be quite cold and standing in formation it's freaking freezing. We may not know what the hell's flying, but the drill sergeants are professionals. Most of them have been through this many times before, so before we know it, we are actually in some sort of formation. Told that neither the people we're with currently nor the accommodations are permanent, but only for the next three days so we shouldn't get too cozy. Our basic training is to last a total of ten weeks, with the first three days being orientation and processing days. After formation, we're taken to breakfast and on the way, we're taught the concept of "double time," which means jogging rather than walking. In the army, walking is considered a waste of time. For the next ten weeks we need to get used to running, marching, and double time.

Since I didn't eat last night, I'm famished. As was attributed to Napoleon Bonaparte, "An army marches on its stomach," and the US Army has taken that to heart. Breakfast is great! Almost every breakfast food you can imagine, and plenty of it. Immediately after breakfast, we're marched over to the base barber shop for a haircut. In basic training you can request any hairstyle you want, but regardless of what you request, we all end up with the same type of haircut, a down-to-the-scalp crew cut, all the way down to the fuzz! If one has a beard, as I do, they don't shave it entirely off, just one half. I learn that this is tradition, and the military barber's sense of humor, along with a strong hint to get rid of the other half. Wow, I never realized how much heat hair provides until I walked out of the barber shop practically bald.

Lots to do and such a short time to do it! Next stop is the quartermaster where we get our uniforms and supplies. In the US military, all of our material needs are taken care of, and for that reason we're told not to bring anything with us. Everything we need is supplied, and I mean everything, from our everyday fatigues to our dress uniforms and even a formal uniform. Nothing is secondhand, everything brand new, hats, jackets, sweaters, socks, and underwear. It's an amazing operation, just like an assembly line at a top-notch factory, with the staff able to estimate your size by just looking at you. Everything is so professional and efficient that even if some type of alteration is needed, it's done on the spot.

At the very end of receiving our uniforms and equipment, we're given boxes and told to put every piece of civilian clothing we have in our possession in the box. Nothing is to be left out, every stitch of clothing, any other personal items, and even our eye glasses if we wear them. The boxes are then sealed and shipped to our homes, which in my case is the fraternity house.

A soldier for only one day, I'm already dreaming about the end of these ten weeks, and graduation day. These first three days are a constant "hurry up and wait" process, in which we take care of everything needed to get us on our way. Going from various orientation sessions to various medical and psychological examinations, I even get myself a couple of pairs of new army-issued eye glasses.

Only my first day. It's simply amazing how much we've accomplished in such a short time, and by the time we get back to the barracks, we're totally exhausted, and training hasn't even started.

Our second day starts out exactly as the first, only today I'm one of the first to be in formation. After breakfast, we double time to a massive building that during the Korean War was an airplane hangar. Upon arrival we're immediately told to strip down to our underwear, which to say the least is a very strange request, but rule number four, obey orders and shut up. It's pretty chilly here, and quite a bit embarrassing as we stand around just waiting. Freezing our buns off, we're finally told that amongst other things, we will be getting a series of immunizations. Ordered to form two lines and wait. As our name is called, we are told to step forward and receive our injections. Like a very professionally run assembly line, the medical staff has us alternating between our right and left arms for the various shots we need to get. It's a bit uncomfortable, but not as uncomfortable as what comes next, which is extremely weird. As our names are called, we're told to yell out our religion. What the hell? There's no way I'm going to do this! I don't know for sure, but I'm willing to bet there aren't too many Jews here. Why do they need to know my religion, and more so, why do I need to yell it out? Strange as it seems, there is a logical explanation. The information is needed for our dog tags. Dog tags are identification tags, the metal discs that a soldier must always wear around his neck. The dog tags consist of one's name, rank, serial number, blood type, and religion. Religion is needed because if, God forbid, you're seriously wounded or killed, they need to know which clergyman is needed to perform last rites. This makes sense, but nonetheless, I'm in total panic! Embarrassment can be worse than death, and this is going to be very embarrassing. All different religions are being yelled out: Catholic, Protestant, Baptist, some even declaring that they're atheist or have no preference at all. I'm petrified! God, please let there be at least one other Jew here, at least one, please! It continues, Catholic, Protestant, no preference, what am I going to do? Okay, that's it, I make a decision. If there are no other Jews before my name is called, I'm going to declare myself as no preference. Finally, my name is called, and being that there seem to be no other Jews, I open my mouth to say no preference, but I just can't. My mind says no preference, but out of my mouth comes Jewish instead. You can hear a pin drop. Over two hundred men, and I'm the only Jew in the bunch.

Our clothes back on, we're given a smoke break. I still haven't quite gotten over the stress of what just transpired, and now I'm in the middle of all this smoking, which is quickly becoming my biggest pet peeve. It's not that I'm against smoking, but after each smoke break, we have to police the area, which means picking up all the cigarette butts, whether one is a smoker or not. Unlike almost all the other trainees here, I don't smoke, but I still have to clean up. The truth is that right now, I wish I did smoke, because as stressed as I am, this would be a great time for a cigarette. Definitely a bit on edge from what just happened, I'm standing off to the side on my lonesome when these two tall, very well-built black guys approach me and ask me if I'm the Jew. Timidly, I answer yes, expecting the worst, but instead of trouble, I see a couple of very warm smiles. Joseph and Leroy tell me that they're both Christians who have always had a love for the Jewish people but never had a real opportunity to meet one of us.

In the US Army, unlike other military services around the world, everyone here, with the exception of a few particular areas like clergymen and doctors, are first and foremost soldiers. The rational being that even if you are in a field that has absolutely nothing to do with combat, you should have the basic skills to fight if the country is ever in an emergency situation where every able-bodied soldier is needed. This being the case, almost everyone starts their military training with basic soldiering skills and basic combat training. If their eventual job will indeed be combat soldiers, then they'll be trained afterward in some sort of advanced combat course. While I'll eventually be trained as a combat nurse, my two new friends are professional musicians. They've been accepted to be part of the elite US Army band and will be stationed in Washington DC. Over the next ten weeks, Joseph and Leroy become my closest friends, even keeping in touch for years afterward.

The third day of orientation is much of the same but closes out with our being assigned to our different training companies.

Assigned to the third brigade, fifth battalion, there are two hundred of us in company A, and we're divided into four platoons of fifty men, with five squads of ten men each. I'm assigned to the second platoon, second squad, and am lucky because both Joseph and Leroy are in the same platoon. Now that we have been assigned to our permanent training company, we are moved to more modern barracks that will be our home for the next ten weeks. Here we are eight to a room instead of twenty-five. Each platoon has three drill sergeants, a senior drill sergeant and two assistants, and our senior drill sergeant is Sergeant First Class Carl Widner. Sergeant Widner lets us know very quickly that we are to refer to him by no other name than Drill Sergeant. What's very unique about Sergeant Widner is that unlike the other drill sergeants, he doesn't have the typical masochistic attitude. In fact, he has been in the army for over twenty years and will be retiring soon. Previously having been stationed in Germany, he's planning after his retirement to go back and open up a house of prostitution, where he says it's legal.

While I know some of my past fears may have been imagined, here my fears are real. Told day in and day out that we're indeed the lowest form of life and beneath contempt, we're either going to become lean, mean fighting soldiers or die trying. Being lower than maggots is not an excuse and is not tolerated. Here, there's no such thing as trying. Trying is for preschoolers, either we do it or we die trying! I really don't know if Sergeant Widner is talking literally or figuratively, but it doesn't matter because every mistake is punished, and almost everything is a mistake.

Most punishment starts with the words "get down and give me" and then it's just a question of how many pushups the drill sergeant decides he wants to give you. It isn't only our own drill sergeants; any of the drill sergeants on the base can and do, and as bad and mean as ours are, the third platoon has some real monsters. Whenever pushups are given, we have to count them off, yelling, one push up Drill Sergeant, two pushups Drill Sergeant, etc. Regardless of how many pushups I'm given to do, I'm never able to do them right. Whether it's Sergeant Widner or some other drill sergeant, they always seem to have a problem hearing me. "I can't hear you", they yell, and I have to start over. Fifty pushups are never just fifty, and they tend to add up very quickly. Without exaggeration I'll probably end up doing close to ten thousand pushups during my basic training. It's not just these extra pushups, our "regular" physical training is very intense with pushups, sit-ups, jumping jacks, running, and plenty of other exercises. All this is not even mentioning the obstacle course and loads of other interesting drills. We're also learning how to use handheld weapons, grenades, mortars, and other weapons of destruction, and I've even been distinguished as a marksman. Training being very intense, we go through many different types of classes and exercises that are meant to turn us into lean, mean fighting machines. We're trained not just with weapons and physically, but also much more. Drill is our main daily activity and is divided into two different types of marching, close order and field. Close order drill is learning to march in a parade formation, learning commands with or without weapons such as standing at attention, at ease, etc. Field marching is basically combat marches. These marches are by no means leisurely hikes. They are hikes and drills that go on in all types of weather, some being as long as thirty miles with full combat gear. Between the thousands of pushups, I'm doing and the drilling, I'm getting more exercise in these ten weeks than probably ever in my life.

I don't know if it is always like this at Fort Leonard Wood, but because of the weather, most of the time we end up marching in mud and marching in mud in combat boots is not fun. Day in and day out, with most Sundays off, this is my existence, and even though Sundays are usually off days, we're still restricted to the base.

We're told that the whole purpose of everything we're going through is to turn us into the best fighting soldiers in the world. On the one hand I would rather go back to being a lowly maggot, but in truth I've got to admit it's a great feeling, knowing that each week we're becoming better and better. Similar to being in prison, with time our privileges grow as well. While Sergeant Widner does not have the mean streak as other drill sergeants, he's still very tough, with certain red lines that one had better not cross. Besides his personal rules, there are other general cardinal rules in the military, in fact any military. The first cardinal rule of any military unit in any country in the world is never to volunteer for anything. A classic example of why not is when a commissioned or noncommissioned officer asks if anybody has a driver's license. Even though this is a well-known gag, there's always someone who falls for it. Why wouldn't I volunteer, if I indeed have a driver's license? Why wouldn't I want a cushy job driving a vehicle? Because chances are that I won't be driving a vehicle but will end up driving something like a wheelbarrow. One of the advantages I have over most of my fellow trainees is that I'm a product of the system, and being that a system is a system, I'm well aware of the games.

Even being a supposed expert on the system, it seems strange to me when one morning at formation, Sergeant Widner asks if anybody knows how to type. For some reason, I answer yes! The truth is that I don't have a clue how to type, but I say yes anyway, and once again God is looking out for me. Sergeant Widner needs a personal flunky, and while being his personal flunky doesn't necessarily mean that I'll get out of training exercises, physical or otherwise, it does get me out of cleaning and kitchen detail. KP (kitchen patrol) and latrine duty are a couple of duties that are a staple of basic training, almost like pushups. Almost nobody manages to get through boot camp without doing one or the other, or usually both. Except me! Sergeant Widner has me doing all of his personal errands, and as my reward I'm exempted from both KP and barracks cleaning. Instead of cleaning the barracks every morning, I'm the latrine queen. I'm in charge of the cleaning closet, which entails being responsible for and handing out all the cleaning supplies used every morning to clean the barracks.

My other reward, which Sergeant Widner isn't aware of, is my off-the-record activity. Because of the different errands he has me doing, I'm sometimes required to go to different places on the base, which allows me to acquire things that nobody else can. Using my street smarts, I've started a little business on the side, running certain errands for my fellow trainees.

Sergeant Widner is an unusual guy in many ways. His biggest pet peeve is racism or prejudice within the ranks. When you first meet him, you think he's a stereotypical WASP (white Anglo Saxon Protestant) who hails from the south with its classic stereotypes. But he's actually quite the opposite, unable to stand for any sort of prejudice. On the first day we meet him, he tells us to look down at our uniform shirts, telling us to read out loud what's written on the right side. US Army, Drill Sergeant! That's what it says, but he responds, wrong! Get down and give me twenty-five. After we do twenty-five pushups, he asks us again and, being really confused, nobody answers. Once again he tells us to get down, this time for fifty pushups. After we're done one hundred pushups, and we think we're dying, he says, never forget this, it doesn't say US Army, it says "us" Army, "us" meaning we're all the same. We're all soldiers, and we have only one color, green! Continuing, he says, there's no black, white, brown, or anything else, only green. This is good news for me, because even though my race is white, I'm also Jewish, and the only Jew here to boot, which definitely puts me in the minority.

Even though I'm very conscious about being the lone Jew in my unit, in truth, I've only felt anti-Semitism twice in my military career. The first is here in basic training. Just like at JINS, there's one guy here who's a real jerk, always muttering some type of anti-Semitic remark under his breath. As in JINS and Edgmead, and every other institution I've been in, one of the most consistent rules is no fighting, and no matter whose fault it is, both parties are subject to punishment, although in the army, punishment is called court martial.

At first, I ignore him, but that only emboldens him. What makes it even more worrisome is that if this kind of thing isn't nipped in the bud, it can become contagious. Unfortunately, most people are sheep and just go along with the crowd. While I get along with most of the guys in my unit, my only two real friends are still Leroy and Joseph, the musicians. I tell them I feel that I'm about to lose my temper and smack this guy in the head. Leroy and Joseph ask me if I want them to take care of my problem. Under normal circumstances, I would happily say yes, seeing that they're both built like brick walls, and just running into them would give you a concussion. In this case, I'm actually afraid to do anything, because I don't want to get in trouble, and I certainly don't want them to get in trouble because of me. Not knowing what to do, after much thinking, I figure that my last resort is to tell Sergeant Widner what's going on. Since I've a good relationship with him, I tell him that I'm afraid I'm going to blow up on this guy and risk a court martial.

As expected, he tells me to ignore the jerk because unlike when one's a regular soldier, the consequences of court martial are much more severe for a trainee. With no other choice, I acquiesce. The following morning, in formation as usual, I notice that my nemesis has an eye that is now black and blue. When others ask him what happened, he replies that he slipped while walking down the stairs. I don't know whether this is true or not, but he never bothers me again.

# Chapter 31

***Believe in yourself and you will be unstoppable.*** —
**Anonymous**

Several days after arriving at boot camp, our unit chaplain looks me up. A Catholic priest who found out I was Jewish, he explains to me that every military unit has a chaplain assigned to it. First Lieutenant Malory is our chaplain, and he's responsible for all our religious and spiritual needs. It doesn't matter what the soldier's religion is, or even if they don't claim a religion at all, if something requires the services of a specific denomination, his job is to get you in touch with the right person. Lieutenant Malory's an extremely nice guy who asks if I have any special requests or needs, specifically do I want kosher food? He explains that since there's a dearth of Jewish personnel in the military, unofficially they're trying to encourage more Jewish enlistment and retention. Most people think I keep kosher, because there are certain foods that I don't eat, but the truth is that I haven't been on a strictly kosher diet in a while. More out of identity and nationalistic reasons, rather than religious conviction, I've been keeping my own version of kosher, meaning definitely not eating pork products and shellfish. On the other hand, if the army is willing to go to bat for me, who am I to say no? In the end, they supply me with kosher food packages and, supplemented with the regular food from the army mess, believe me, I never go hungry. The only time food is a little bit of a challenge is when we're out in the field on maneuvers. On bivouac, it's not just me and my kosher food, it's all of us. While food in the mess is pretty good, out in the field it can be hit or miss. Although sometimes they do bring out hot food to us in the field, usually it's C-Rations. The C-Ration is now officially called the Meal Combat Individual (MCI), but it's still very similar to the original, and everybody still calls them C-Rations.

Missouri winters can be very cold, sometimes getting into the below-zero range, and sleeping in a tent can be very uncomfortable. It's a particularly cold day, and we're in the middle of a three-day battle simulation, when the chow truck arrives. Not a big coffee drinker, I usually decline, but being that it's really cold, I grab my mess cup for a fill up. Finding myself almost instinctively placing the cup between my legs, I think about Abba. I remember that whenever my father had a hot beverage in his hand, he would repeat the same story. Reminiscing, he would start by saying, did I ever tell you about when I was in the army? And then he would proceed to tell us. During World War II, in freezing cold weather, they'd bring coffee around, and even though he didn't drink coffee, he'd still always take one, placing the cup between his legs to keep himself warm. Taking the coffee, I look over at Leroy and I say to him, Leroy, did I ever tell you the story?

No other words to describe it, basic training is tough! Up before dawn, by the time we hit the pillow at night we're out like a light. Mentally and physically exhausted, some nights we don't even get to sleep through the night because of the many maneuvers or night drills we have. Sleep is the most valuable commodity in basic training. Some nights we get just a couple hours of sleep, so every minute of sleep is precious, but besides everything else, there's always fire watch. Most things in boot camp have some type of logical rational, but fire watch is just a mind game. Supposedly one person in each barracks has to be awake at all times, to watch out for fire or some other calamity. What this means is a two-hour rotation nightly, with each of us getting hit with fire watch about once every couple of weeks. The origins of fire watch goes back to the time when there were actually open fire stoves heating the barracks, and there was indeed a fire hazard. As well, somebody was always needed to make sure that the fire didn't go out during the night. Always seeming to have the luck of the Irish, on one of my tours the clocks are changing to spring time, so I end up doing only one hour rather than two. I feel sorry for the poor guy who does his training in the fall, who'd end up doing an extra hour.

As the weeks go by, I'm feeling the changes, both physically and mentally. Now doing more pushups than I could've ever imagined, I'm also running up to ten miles a day. We're all feeling very proud, and we can see that slowly but surely, we're turning into real soldiers. Even Sergeant Widner seems impressed by our progress.

Passover is coming up, and while Fort Leonard Wood doesn't have a permanent Jewish chaplain, one is scheduled to arrive for the holiday. Captain Thomas, our company commander, lets me know that if I want to, I can get a furlough and go home for all of Passover. Either that or stay on and be excused from certain duties. The challenge is that if I take leave now, I won't be able to graduate with my unit and may in fact have to do basic training all over again. Deciding to stay, I attend Passover Seder on base, which is being hosted for the few Jewish personnel stationed here, one of whom happens to be a general.

Passover night, colloquially known as Seder night, I'm feeling a little nervous as just a lowly trainee, but it's hard not to see the humor when I think about where my buddies are. Tonight they're out in the pouring rain on a bivouac exercise, while here I am, sitting next to General Reisner, a three-star general, and having a real conversation.

It's now a week before our training is complete, and they're drilling us day and night, getting us ready for our commencement ceremony. A busy week, with all sorts of movement going on as plans are being made and orders are being cut. Most of the soldiers in my unit are on regular active duty and will be going straight to their next training assignments. The rest of us, who are either in the reserves or in some special program as I am, all have different arrangements.

For a few months, I'll be heading back to Boise to continue my studies, then on to my next assignment, at Fort Sam Houston in San Antonio, Texas. As part of the separation process, I'm called into a meeting with Sergeant Widner and Captain Thomas. Even though I already have a commitment to the military, it's still a type of sales job. They want to discuss my future vis-a-vis the military, and I'm really surprised, because they're both trying to convince me to change career directions. Rather than going into nursing, they're suggesting I go to divinity school, get my rabbinical ordination, and return to the army as a military chaplain. I cannot for the life of me understand why they think I'd make a good chaplain. As they're both being quite insistent, I tell them I'll consider it, even though I've absolutely no interest. The truth is that even if I did, there's no way, with my lack of education and criminal background, I'd be able to get *Semicha* (rabbinical ordination). As far as I'm concerned, it's more realistic that I go play center for a professional basketball team than become a rabbi, and I'm only five and a half feet tall.

**There's a Jewish proverb that Man plans, and God laughs. In this case, I laughed, and God planned. Thirty years later, as part of my mid-life crisis, I went back to school and received my rabbinical ordination.**

Today is graduation day. Many people are under the misconception that completing basic training is a given, but it's not. The latest statistics show that close to 20 percent of recruits don't make it and end up getting tossed out of the Army. Basic training has taught us the basic military customs, along with the necessary training to equip us to serve our country as part of the United States Military. Part of being in the military involves tradition, and the formal graduation ceremony is a big part of it. In fact, for many, families and friends come from all over the country to witness the final transformation of their recruit from an everyday citizen to a soldier in the U.S. Army. I don't expect to see anybody there for me, but I know I have friends and family who are proud of my accomplishments.

These past ten weeks have been one of the hardest things I've ever done in my life. It's difficult to believe what just ten weeks can do to a person, and although I never want to repeat it again, I'm so proud of myself that I did it.

# Chapter 32

*Let me tell you this: if you meet a loner, no matter what they tell you, it's not because they enjoy solitude. It's because they have tried to blend into the world before, and people continue to disappoint them.* —Jodi Picoult

Back in Boise, and with my priorities changing, I'm no longer living in the fraternity house. I've moved into an apartment off campus with a classmate of mine. Felix, a pretty fastidious guy, is quite the opposite of me. I'm not exactly the most organized person in the world. In fact, I'm rather a mess. I'm also confused and lonely.

I feel like I'm all alone in this world. On the one hand, I'm really blessed with loads of friends, yet when all by myself, I stress out. It makes no sense: I've accomplished so much and have everything to be proud of. Well liked, plenty of friends, articulate, and on the face of it, I've blended well into society, pretty much like everyone else.

No one truly knows another person's reality. The only reality any person can experience is the one that's in one's thoughts and conscience. Not realizing what or why, I can't shake feelings of rejection and abandonment. I'm scared as hell. Of legal age now so no longer under the auspices of my parents or the authorities, I can do what I want, when I want, so why am I so bummed? Maybe that's just it—who's going to take care of me now?

Even though everything in my life seems perfect, I'm a basket case, and even though I'm usually good at hiding my feelings, this time my friends notice a change. Everyone thinks that my experience in boot camp changed me, and while that's partially true, I'm just lost, and I don't know how to find myself.

I've got so many stories and incidents in my life, but right now one of them stands out. I'm about eight years old, living in Laurelton, and as little boys sometimes will do, I'm playing with matches. By accident, I drop one of the lighted matches into my wastepaper basket, causing it to catch on fire. Freaked out by the flames, I take one of my sneakers and use it to stamp out the fire. Although the fire is out, I now have a smoldering sneaker, and not knowing what to do, I toss it out the window. Several minutes later, I hear my father racing through the house yelling, does anybody else smell smoke? Keeping my mouth shut and playing dumb, I certainly don't. Feeling the walls and looking around, Abba is sure something's on fire but can't find anything. He calls the fire department, asking them just for advice. He tells them, no reason for you to come, just tell me what to look for. While he's still on the phone, I can hear the sirens of the firetrucks blaring in the distance, and within a few minutes, there are a dozen firemen running through our house. It doesn't take long until the fire chief walks into the house, holding my smoldering sneaker. Looking at my father, he says, if it was my son, I know what I'd do… Abba gives me a whipping that night, and maybe I deserve it. But it isn't the whipping that hurts as much as what he says afterward: You're a nothing and will always be a nothing! I know he doesn't mean it, he's just frustrated by my shenanigans and doesn't know what else to do. I had never felt lonelier than right at that moment, and that's how I feel right now.

At the beginning of August, I head to San Antonio, Texas, for my next phase of military training, and this is where I start to learn about combat medicine. Fort Sam Houston, colloquially known as "Fort Sam," acts, amongst other things, as the command headquarters of the Army Medical Command and the Army Medical Department Center and School, and is to be my home for the next few months.

Being back in a stable environment is good for me. Very busy with intense courses, I learn and study hard, quickly jumping to the top of the class. Feeling really good being back in the Army, life here is much different than during boot camp. Training is still very tough, and it's certainly much harder academically than basic training, but here, we're no longer scum and maggots. Being a cadet has its privileges, and if we're not in training, being punished for something or another, or on duty, we're free to go and come as we please.

Academically, I'm doing fantastic; who would've thought? Almost every day is a good day for me, and I'm even considering making the military a career, but that's getting ahead of myself. I've still got lots of ground to cover, and right now, I've just got to keep my nose to the grindstone and keep studying. It's really intense, with exams every other day. If you fail a test, you're given one shot at a makeup. Failing a second time, you're out of the program. My mother always used to tell me, busy is good, and I see here what she was talking about.

As the months have flown by, I've hardly had any time to think, which in my case is really good. Before I know it, the year is coming to an end, and I'm entitled to a three-week furlough. Never believing that I'd have a hard time making this decision, I now have to choose if I want to spend it in Boise or go home to Elizabeth. I decide to split my time, going first to Boise, where I spend Christmas with Eddie and his family, and then to Elizabeth where I spend New Year's Day and my nineteenth birthday. My vacation now over, I've new orders cut. Instead of returning to Fort Sam, I'm directed to report to Fort Carson, which is right outside of Colorado Springs. Fort Carson is the home to a number of different units, like the Fourth Infantry Division, the Tenth Special Forces Group, and the Tenth Combat Support Hospital, which is where I'm assigned. This is supposed to be what's referred to in military slang as TDY, temporary duty assignment, and I'm supposed to be here just a couple of months for further training.

The year is 1980, and the United States is not doing well on the diplomatic or military front. Iran is currently holding fifty-two Americans hostage in the US Embassy in Tehran. Not knowing if the current situation has anything to do with anything, my training gets more intensive, and my stay at Fort Carson is extended.

Scrunched up with about fifteen other guys in the back of an MC-130E Combat Talon, we're heading toward some unknown destination. This is the last place I'm supposed to be. After all, there's no draft, nobody put a gun to my head. What am I doing here? And what the hell have I gotten myself into?

I'm really not supposed to be here. Most of the people I know think I'm nuts for doing this, but I'm really proud of myself. I'm doing something different, something patriotic, which is unusual in my social circles. Maybe they're right, but then again, I've always been an oddball. In fact, by all rights I should be dead, or rotting in prison. Maybe tonight I'll die, but even if I do, I'll die a hero, and that'll show 'em!

Mission aborted, yells the lieutenant. What? Why? What's going on? No further information, mission's been scrubbed, we're heading home…

# Chapter 33

## *It ain't over till it's over.* —Yogi Berra

It would be really great to say that my life is smooth sailing from here on out, but life doesn't work that way. In many ways, my life has become even more difficult, because I no longer have any excuses.

So yes, I've reached adulthood, and on the face of it, I've beaten the odds. Becoming a productive member of society, which in itself is pretty amazing, is something I should definitely be proud of. In reality though, I'm starting now from perhaps not the exact same position that I started those many years ago, but not so far off. The difference being simply one of age.

In spite of my apparent success, I'm once again behind that same proverbial eight ball, but this time it seems even worse. Maybe because I'm older and already understand what it means to start out behind the eight ball, or maybe because it's indeed worse. Either way, I'm lacking in some of the most basic life and social skills, which one needs in my socioeconomic circles.

An expert in street and survival skills, if that was my world, I'd be all set, but my world is the normal world. My world is the middle-to–upper-class world, and although I may know how to fake it in this world, I certainly don't know how to make it. Even worse, a child gets a certain amount of sympathy for being all alone. I'm no longer a child.

Yea, right now I'm doing okay, even really good. In university and the Army, I've almost all my financial needs being taken care of, but I'm still scared about what comes next. Already worrying about the future, I realize that one of my major afflictions is no stability. I'm always worried about tomorrow, never able to enjoy the present. Always worried that at any moment the bottom will fall through, and many times, I manage to fulfil my own self-fulfilling prophecies.

This book is not meant to be about doom and gloom, in fact it's meant to be quite the opposite. Starting life with all the odds in my favor, I quickly found myself behind the eight ball. I suffered, struggled, and persevered until I finally won. But I only won the battle, not the war. The war is far from over. As the saying goes, it ain't over till the fat lady sings, and the fat lady only sings once you transition to the world above. There's a concept of life known as the four S's: Survival, Stability, Success, and Significance, but Stability continues to elude me. It's a general concept that everyone is raised through their developmental years within one of these S boxes. On the face of it, I should've left those years with perhaps Success under my belt, but certainly Stability. Instead, I left with Survival.

Sometimes we see someone successful, perhaps one who enjoys fame and fortune. We may be tempted to think that it came to them easily, as some sort of a gift, or that they were born with it. The truth is, most really successful people work very hard for their success. The only advantage they may have is that most have probably learnt Success or Significance skills in their developmental years, but almost for sure Stability. For instance, let's take the current president of the United States, who most people would agree was not born with the presidential mantle. What he did have was the right life skills, so when he made the decision to run for president, he was already halfway there. That being said, while he may have learned Success skills, he worked hard to get to the next level, that of Significance.

We see this journey everywhere in life: relationships, business/work, health, etc., but not everybody gets to Significance in their lifetime, and unfortunately, most people don't even manage to master Survival. Although the majority of the world never even makes it to Stability, regardless of where you start out, it's still possible to go from Survival to Significance. The most important thing in the four S's journey is to make a decision to grow. It doesn't make any difference how old you are, or at what stage you are in life. It can take a short time or a very long time, and although we can't make a conclusive judgment on the final S of a person until after their death, we each more or less know exactly where we are at any given stage of our lives.

That being said, can anyone get to whichever stage they want? Let's take for example a woman who grows up in the deep, dark jungles of the Amazon. While nothing is impossible, realistically, what are her chances of achieving Stability, let alone Success in the Western world? Slim to none! But can she reach Significance in her society? Why not? Everything is relative in the world of the four S's, and the final word is up to you. You know where you are and where you want to get to. Don't let others judge you, and don't allow yourself to be judged.

Referring to life skills, while I believe it's easy for most of us to grasp the concept, we tend to think about the big ones. Forget about the big ones. It's always the little stuff that messes us up. Stick to working on the small stuff, and the big stuff will take care of itself.

Most basic skills are taken for granted, because we usually learn them as a child and aren't even aware of it. Some are actually not even technically taught, but in fact are formed by some sort of osmosis. A perfect example is tying one's shoelaces. Seems pretty simple but imagine meeting an adult who doesn't know how to tie his or her shoelaces. What would you think? Surely something's wrong with them, perhaps they're stupid or mentally challenged, but definitely something's out of whack. Could you even entertain the possibility that perhaps no one ever taught them the simple act of tying their shoelaces?

Of course, there may be any number of reasons as to why he doesn't know how to tie his shoelaces. Perhaps he grew up without ever owning laced shoes, after all there are other types of shoes; Velcro, slip on, buckle, etc. Nonetheless, we would definitely think something was odd. But again, I ask you to entertain the possibility that he was never taught.

Are you, as a shoelace expert, able to entertain the possibility that this person is anything but odd?

Now, as the guy who doesn't know how to tie his shoelaces, we've an added challenge! The older we get, the harder it is for us to admit that we simply might not know something. Especially when everyone else looks at it as a no-brainer. So, we become arrogant or defensive or we start feeling sorry for ourselves. Suffering in silence, we put up with the ridicule, but ashamed as we are, we're more ashamed to ask for help.

How much different—and I submit, better—would our lives be if at the age of let's say, thirty, forty, fifty years old, we were willing to admit that we never learned to tie our shoelaces and asked someone to teach us? Nowadays, it's so much easier to learn things than ever before, with the advent of the internet. But even with Google or YouTube, it's still amazing how many people are afraid to move out of their box and ask for help.

Not having been taught some of these basic life skills, my life was really hampered growing up, which destroyed much of my self-esteem. Even though at some point I started enjoying a bit of success, it was too late for me. Reaching adulthood, it got even worse, because as an adult I was no longer given the benefit of the doubt. No longer a child, I was "expected" to know things. Many times throughout my adult life, people who had problems with me because of my actions or lack thereof would automatically think I was dumb, stupid, or lazy. Responding in my defense that I was simply never taught this or that, they'd look at me incredulously and say, give me a break, everyone knows how to do _____. When I went through basic training, most of my colleagues had never before made a bed in their entire lives. Did that make them dumb, stupid, or lazy? I, on the other hand, had been taught this skill in my past incarceration experiences. Did that make me better or smarter than the others? No, it just meant that I had already learnt that particular skill.

# Chapter 34

*Determination gives you the resolve to keep going in spite of the roadblocks that lay before you.* —**Denis Waitley**

In spite of it all, I made it. I reached adulthood. Looking back at my childhood, I have to admit that it wasn't all bad; in fact there were some good times. That said, almost all my experiences came with mixed emotions, with some of my experiences being very scary and harrowing. The emotional scars I carry may never go away, and I've given up trying to make them. Life is too short, and I'm more interested in the future than the past. It's irrelevant who was to blame; these are the cards I was dealt, and my job is just to play them the best I can. As painful as the past may have been, I can't escape from the fact that many of the terrible things I experienced molded me into the person that I am today, and I love who I am today.

In spite of it all, I've never been happier, and today I love myself and my life.

In spite of it all, I know how blessed I am to have the friends and family that I do.

In spite of it all, I've met tons of unbelievable people throughout the years, that if I'd been "normal," I may never have had the opportunity to know.

In spite of it all, I've learnt and experienced things that most people can only dream about.

In spite of it all, I've touched more people and helped more people improve their lives than I could've ever imagined.

And in spite of it all, I still like to have the occasional pity party, but so what.

Although I'm a traditional God believer, nothing else is traditional about me. The traditional heaven and hell scenario doesn't fit into my lexicon. I believe that this place, this earth, is heaven or hell, and it's completely up to us. God loves us, and the definition of God is pure love. There is no such thing as bad in God, nor in God's world; everything here is great! Pretty wild thinking, huh? Look at what goes on around us daily in this world. How can I make such a bold statement? In fact, after everything you've just read about my childhood, it might seem a pretty absurd statement. Let me try and explain.

We all have our mission in this life. None of us know what it is when we start out, and few of us are fortunate to know even at the end of our lives. Yet, we still have our mission, and in order to complete our mission, we have to grow and blossom in a certain way. We're all not born the same: some of us are born apples, and some oranges. Some of us are born tomatoes, some cucumbers, and some corn on the cob. Regardless of the type of fruit or vegetable we are, we have two things in common. First, we were all created in the image of God, and second, we all have been assigned a personal mission to complete. Whether or not we complete our mission is totally up to us! We have no choice in the type of fruit or vegetable we are, nor what cards we are dealt, but we all have a choice in how we play those cards today, and what we do with the rest of our lives.

Almost everything in life is a choice, although many times we believe it's out of our hands. The truth is that hardly anything in our life is out of our hands. Shakespeare was quoted as saying that "all the world is a stage, and all the men and women merely players." Shakespeare, while not normally a positive person, almost got it right. I not only believe, I'm convinced that we're the star players in each of our individual plays. Everybody we come in contact with, whomever we interact with, is here at our behest. Whether they're a bit player or a major actor, they're here for one reason only: to serve us! We all have our mission in life, we've all been given the tools to accomplish that mission, and it's entirely up to us. That being said, while we might not know what our mission is when we start out in life, and perhaps not even at the end of our lives, nonetheless, we all have a choice. Moment by moment, day by day, whether or not we complete that mission is totally up to us.

There's a rare disease referred to as congenital analgesia. Congenital analgesia is an insensitivity to pain that inhibits the ability to perceive physical pain. From birth, affected individuals never feel pain in any part of their body. People with this condition can feel the difference between sharp and dull, and hot and cold, but they cannot sense, for example, that a hot beverage is burning their tongue. This lack of pain awareness often leads to an accumulation of wounds, bruises, broken bones, and other health issues that may go undetected. So, in other words, these people don't feel pain, but the damage is still done. For instance, imagine putting your hand into a roaring campfire and not feeling any pain. Good or bad? Good, I guess, because there's no pain. Yes, no pain, but what about the irreparable damage? If you let it stay in the fire long enough, you may lose your hand. So maybe pain is not so bad. Nobody likes pain and suffering, whether it's emotional or physical. The question simply is, will we benefit from this pain or not? I have a terrific life right now. It's fantastic! Would I be here without my past suffering and pain? I think not! Does this mean I enjoyed the pain or am happy that I had to suffer? If I say yes, that would make me a masochist or a pathological liar.

Living life every day to its fullest, I don't worry about the past. I only use the past if it can help me in the present, and the future I tend not to think much about at all. I know that if I take care of today, chances are that tomorrow will be as good or better. In fact, let me ask you a question. If today has been a fantastic day for you, where everything has gone wonderfully, just the way you like it, what are the chances that tomorrow will be at least as good, if not better?

On the other hand, imagine today has been a terrible day for you, a really, really lousy day. Everything that could go wrong, went wrong. What are the chances that tomorrow will be at least as bad, if not worse?

So, if you're having a good day today, expect the same, and that chances are excellent that tomorrow will be as good or better. If you have a bad day today, go to bed as early as possible. Before you do, though, read or listen to something positive, or listen to some good relaxing music. Whatever you do, don't read the newspaper or watch television. Finally, expect that tomorrow will be good, and chances are that it will certainly be better than today. Even if tomorrow doesn't turn out to be your best day, if you follow this formula, I promise you that your life will only get better and better.

This is a system that works! It's simple logic: the more good days you have, the more good days you will have. Unfortunately, the reverse is just as true. It took me many, many years to learn to strive for only good days, and while not every day is good, I would venture to say that 90 percent of my days are not just good, but fantastic.

I wrote this book for you! Yes, you! You know exactly who I'm referring to, so don't look to the left or the right. You know I'm talking about you! Today is the first day of the rest of your life, so make it the best day ever, because nothing else is as important as you, and today…

www.ingramcontent.com/pod-product-compliance
Lightning Source LLC
Chambersburg PA
CBHW031157270326
41931CB00006B/310